1838	15,000 Cherokee Indians forcibly removed from Georgia to Oklahoma make a 1,000-mile "Trail of Tears"
1846–1868	U.S.—Mexican War
1848	California gold rush begins
1848-1885	Construction of the Washington Monument
1849	Harriet Tubman escapes from slavery
1850	Congress passes Fugitive Slave Act; Underground Railroad intensifies
1851	Herman Melville's *Moby Dick*—originally titled *The Whale*—is published
1852	Harriet Beecher Stowe publishes *Uncle Tom's Cabin*; sells 1,000,000 copies
1855	Walt Whitman publishes *Leaves of Grass*
1857	U.S. Supreme Court rules against Dred Scott's suit for freedom
1861	February 4: Southern States form their own confederacy April 12: Confederate forces attack Fort Sumter; Civil War begins
1863	January 1: President Lincoln signs Emancipation Proclamation July 1-3: Battle of Gettysburg November 19: Lincoln gives Gettysburg Address
1865	April 9: Confederate forces surrender at Appomattox April 14: John Wilkes Booth assassinates President Lincoln 13th Amendment abolishes slavery and involuntary servitude
1867	Alaska Purchase: America buys Alaska from Russia for 2 cents an acre
1867–1870	Reconstruction Acts rejoin Southern states to the Union
1868	Louisa May Alcott publishes *Little Women*
1871	Great Chicago Fire levels the city
1876	Alexander Graham Bell invents the telephone Mark Twain publishes *The Adventures of Tom Sawyer* June 25: Sioux and Cheyenne defeat Custer in Battle of the Little Bighorn
1879	Thomas Edison invents the lightbulb
1881	July 2: Charles Guiteau mortally shoots President James Garfield First skyscraper (10 stories) built in Chicago
1886	Coca-Cola hits the market Statue of Liberty is dedicated in New York Harbor
1888	Kodak box camera is introduced
1889	May 30: Johnstown, Pennsylvania flood kills 2,209
1890	December 29: soldiers massacre more than 200 Sioux at Wounded Knee in South Dakota

(continued on rear flaps)

THIS BOOK BELONGS TO:

_____

_____

_____

_____

The LITTLE BIG BOOK of
AMERICA

EDITED BY **Lena Tabori**
& **Natasha Fried**

DESIGNED BY **Jon Glick**

welcome
BOOKS

New York ★ San Francisco

Published in 2002 by Welcome Books,
An imprint of Welcome Enterprises, Inc.
6 West 18 Street, New York, NY 10011
(212) 989-3200; Fax (212) 989-3205
e-mail: info@welcomebooks.biz
www.welcomebooks.biz

Publisher: Lena Tabori
Project Director: Natasha Tabori Fried
Designer: Jon Glick
Recipes: Lena Tabori
Facts: Rachel Hertz
Additional fact-checking, copyediting & timeline: Jana Martin
Editorial assistants: Lawrence Chesler, Deidra Garcia

Distributed to the trade in the U.S. and Canada by
Andrews McMeel Distribution Services
Order Department and Customer Service (800) 223-2336
Orders Only Fax: (800) 943-9831

Library of Congress Control Number: 2002024973

Printed in Singapore
First Edition
2 4 6 8 10 9 7 5 3 1

CONTENTS

LETTERS

SONGS

HISTORICAL DOCUMENTS

RECIPES

FACTS

INTRODUCTION

My love of American history comes from my father. He wasn't an academic, but he was a history buff. Self-educated (he never finished high school), he culled most of his knowledge from documentaries, movies, biographies and articles. It is in this tradition of discovering our heritage and history through secondary sources that I approached the task of editing this book. As my own self-education deepened during the course of my research, it became increasingly clear that I had a lot to learn. About what it means to be the child of immigrants. About how very personal our national history is. And about what it means to be an American.

Learn I did. My first lesson was to accept a frustrating reality. There was no way to fit everything in this book that belongs here, and in the end, that's ok. This isn't the final word on America, but it is a celebration of what's great about this country. The highlights are here. We've got Patrick Henry's "give me liberty or give me death" and Martin Luther King Jr.'s "I Have a Dream." We've got the U.S. Constitution, the opening of Harper Lee's *To Kill A Mockingbird* and Maya Angelou's "America." And we've got facts. Want to know who all of our presidents were and when they served? It's in here. State capitals? Famous American villains? That's here too.

There are surprises, as well. Material I hope you'll be excited to come across. Discover settler William Cobbett's less-than-enthusiastic review of the New World, a recipe for the best Apple Pie and a map of the oddest-named towns in America.

This book works as a quick reference, but it's also a great read. It tells the story of America, through the words of our finest writers, politicians, poets and storytellers. It's interesting, heartwarming and above all, inspiring. My dad was a tough critic, but he would have loved this book. I hope you will too.

Natasha Tabori Fried

POWHATAN TO CAPTAIN JOHN SMITH

JAMESTOWN, VIRGINIA, 1609

Despite the life-saving aid that Powhatan Confederacy tribes gave the first English settlers in Jamestown, the settlers abused the friendship. Conflicts arose over land and the trading of weapons and food. Powhatan (Chief Wahunsonacock), chief of the Powhatan Confederacy and the father of Pocahontas, addressed Captain John Smith with this warning.

I AM NOW GROWN OLD, and must soon die; and the succession must descend, in order, to my brothers, Opitchapan, Opekankanough, and Catataugh, and then to my two sisters, and their two daughters. I wish their experience was equal to mine; and that your love to us might not be less than ours to you.

Why should you take by force that from us which you can have by love? Why should you destroy us, who have provided you with food? What can you get by war? We can hide our provisions, and fly into the woods; and then you must consequently famish by wronging your friends. What is the cause of your jealousy? You see us unarmed, and willing to supply your wants, if you will come in a friendly manner, and not with swords and guns, as to invade an enemy.

I am not so simple, as not to know it is better to eat good meat, lie well, and sleep quietly with my women and children; to laugh and be merry with the English; and, being their friend, to have copper, hatchets, and whatever else I want, than to fly from all, to lie cold in the woods, feed upon acorns, roots, and such trash, and to be so hunted, that I cannot rest, eat, or sleep. In such circumstances, my men must watch, and if a twig should but break, all would cry out, "Here comes Captain Smith"; and so, in this miserable manner, to end my miserable life; and, Captain Smith, this might be soon your fate too, through your rashness and unadvisedness.

I, therefore, exhort you to peaceable councils; and, above all, I insist that the guns and swords, the cause of all our jealousy and uneasiness, be removed and sent away.

AMAZING GRACE

TRADITIONAL HYMN, 1760

Amazing grace, how sweet the sound
That saved a wretch like me
I once was lost, but now I'm found;
Was blind, but now I see.

* * *

Through many dangers, toils and snares
I have already come
It's Grace that brought me safe thus far,
And Grace will lead me home.

When we've been there a thousand years
Bright shining as the sun
We've no less days to sing God's praise
Than when we've first begun.

Apple Pie

pple Pie was originally created by English settlers as a variation on the English meat pie. I discovered this extraordinary version at *Zin* in Sonoma County, California. Chef Jeff Mall explained that the recipe belonged to his mother, Barbara McBride. It is a perennial on his menu.

Piecrust

2 cups sifted all-purpose flour

1 -teaspoon salt

²/₃ cup solid vegetable shortening, chilled

6–8 tablespoons ice water

1. Sift the flour and salt together into a mixing bowl. Cut the vegetable shortening into the flour with a pastry blender (or two knives), until the mixture resembles coarse meal.

2. Sprinkle the ice water in a little at a time, blending it quickly into the dough.

3. Wrap the dough lightly in waxed paper and place it in the refrigerator for 30 minutes.

Pie Filling

5 Gravenstein apples, peeled, cut in half, and sliced 1/2″ thick

2/3 cup sugar

3 tablespoons ground cinnamon

about 2 tablespoons lime juice (1 or 2 limes, juiced)

3 tablespoons "Laird's Apple Jack" apple brandy

1/2 stick unsalted butter, diced

1 tablespoon heavy cream

sugar for dusting pie crust

1. Preheat oven to 400° F.

2. Divide the dough in half, roll out the bottom piecrust, and place in a 9″ round pie plate.

3. Place a third of the apples on the piecrust. Sprinkle with a third of the sugar, 1 teaspoon ground cinnamon, 1 tablespoon lime juice, and 1 tablespoon apple brandy. Dot the apples with a third of the diced butter. Repeat, starting with the rest of the apples.

4. Roll out the top piecrust and place over the top of the pie. Crimp the edges together, and poke steam vents in the top of the pie.

5. Brush the top with cream, sprinkle it with sugar, and place the pie on a cookie sheet. Slide it into the preheated oven.

6. Bake at 400° F for 15–20 minutes until filling starts to bubble.

7. Lower the heat to 350° F and cook for 20 minutes more.

Let the pie cool slightly and serve with vanilla ice cream.

Serves 6 to 8.

The American Revolution

✳

The Boston Tea Party—a protest against British taxes and Britain's monopoly on the tea trade on December 16th of 1773—involved colonists boarding British ships dressed as Mohawk Indians and dumping 342 crates of tea into Boston Harbor. What sort of tea? Darjeeling.

✳

A leader in the American Revolution, Samuel Adams (1722–1803) was a founder of the Sons of Liberty, organized the Boston Tea Party and signed the Declaration of Independence.

✳

As an express rider for the Massachusetts Committee of Safety, silversmith Paul Revere (1734–1818) took two heroic rides. During the first—in December 1774— he warned New Hampshire of a potential British landing.

✳

Immortalized in verse by Longfellow, Revere's more famous ride took place April 18, 1775, when he raced to Lexington to warn that the British were headed for Concord. He was caught, but fellow rider William Dawes made it through. When the British arrived, the Minutemen were there to meet them. The shots fired began the war.

✳

Patriot, lawyer and Virginia governor Patrick Henry (1736–1799) uttered the words "Give me liberty or give me death," and was largely responsible for correcting the new Constitution's shortcomings with the Bill of Rights.

✳

Thomas Jefferson's first draft of the Declaration of Independence included a passage blaming George III for the slave trade. Congress struck it out.

Founding father Alexander Hamilton (1757–1804), the country's first treasury secretary, was killed in a duel with political opponent Aaron Burr.

Seamstress Betsy Ross (1752–1836) was asked by George Washington to sew the first American flag in May, 1776. The original little resembles the current flag, but the stars and stripes were present from the beginning.

It's said that John Hancock (1737–1793) made his signature on the Declaration of Independence big enough for the British king to read without putting on his glasses.

After the war, Noah Webster (1758–1843) created the first genuinely American Dictionary: *A Compendious Dictionary of the English Language* (1806).

Though we celebrate on July 4th, the colonies actually voted for independence July 2, 1776, and the Declaration of Independence wasn't signed by all members of Congress until August 2.

The war ended October 19, 1781, in Yorktown, Virginia. There, Lord Cornwallis surrendered to George Washington and French General Comte de Rochambeau.

GIVE ME LIBERTY OR GIVE ME DEATH

PATRICK HENRY, RICHMOND, VIRGINIA, MARCH 23, 1775

*Patrick Henry, a self-taught lawyer, stood up before a meeting
of 122 delegates and virtually galvanized the room into revolution.*

MR. PRESIDENT, it is natural to man to indulge in the
illusions of hope. We are apt to shut our eyes against a painful
truth, and listen to the song of that siren till she transforms us into
beasts. Is this the part of wise men, engaged in a great and arduous
struggle for liberty? Are we disposed to be of the number of those
who, having eyes, see not, and, having ears, hear not, the things
which so nearly concern their temporal salvation? For my part,
whatever anguish of spirit it may cost, I am willing to know the
whole truth, to know the worst, and to provide for it....

Sir, we have done everything that could be done, to avert the
storm which is now coming on. We have petitioned, we have
remonstrated, we have supplicated, we have prostrated ourselves
before the throne, and have implored its interposition to arrest the
tyrannical hands of the ministry and parliament. Our petitions
have been slighted, our remonstrances have produced additional

violence and insult, our supplications have been disregarded, and we have been spurned with contempt from the foot of the throne! In vain, after these things, may we indulge the fond hope of peace and reconciliation. There is no longer any room for hope. If we wish to be free, if we mean to preserve inviolate those inestimable privileges for which we have been so long contending, if we mean not basely to abandon the noble struggle in which we have been so long engaged, and which we have pledged ourselves never to abandon until the glorious object of our contest shall be obtained, we must fight! I repeat it, sir, we must fight! An appeal to arms and to the God of Hosts is all that is left us.

They tell us, sir, that we are weak, unable to cope with so formidable an adversary. But when shall we be stronger? Will it be the next week or the next year? Will it be when we are totally disarmed, and when a British guard shall be stationed in every house? Shall we gather strength by irresolution and inaction? Shall we acquire the means of effectual resistance, by lying supinely on our backs, and hugging the delusive phantom of hope until our enemies shall have bound us hand and foot? Sir, we are not weak, if we make proper use of those means which the God of nature hath placed in our power. Three millions of people, armed in the holy cause of liberty, and in such a country as that which we possess, are invincible by any force which our enemy can send against us. Besides, sir, we shall not fight our battles alone. There is a just God who presides over the destinies of nations, and who will raise up friends to fight our battles for us. The battle, sir, is not to the strong alone; it is to the vigilant, the active, the brave. Besides, sir, we have no election. If we were base enough to desire it, it is now too late to retire from the contest. There is no retreat but in submission and slavery! Our chains are forged! Their clanking may be heard on the plains of Boston! The war is inevitable—and let it come! I repeat, sir, let it come!

It is in vain, sir, to extenuate the matter. Gentlemen may cry, Peace, Peace, but there is no peace. The next gale that sweeps from the north will bring to our ears the clash of resounding arms! Our brethren are already in the field! Why stand we here idle? What is it that gentlemen wish? What would they have? Is life so dear, or peace so sweet, as to be purchased at the price of chains and slavery? Forbid it, Almighty God! I know not what course others may take, but as for me, give me liberty or give me death!

Yankee Doodle
came to town.

YANKEE DOODLE

ANONYMOUS, 1775

Father and I went down to camp
Along with Captain Goodwin,
And there we saw the men and boys
As thick as hasty pudding.

Chorus
Yankee Doodle, keep it up,
Yankee Doodle dandy!
Mind the music and the steps,
And with the girls be handy!

There was Captain Washington
Upon a slapping stallion,
Giving orders to his men,
I guess there was a million.

And there they had a swamping gun
As big as a log of maple,

On a deuced little cart,
A load for father's cattle.

And every time they fired it off,
It took a horn of powder;
It made a noise like father's gun,
Only a nation louder.

And there I saw a little keg,
Its heads were made of leather—
They knocked upon it with little sticks
To call the folks together.

The troopers, too, would gallop up
And fire right in our faces,
It scared me almost half to death
To see them run such races.

But I can't tell you half I saw;
They kept up such a smother,
So I took off my hat, made a bow,
And scampered home to mother.

GEORGE WASHINGTON
TO MARTHA WASHINGTON

PHILADELPHIA, JUNE 18, 1775

*When the American Rebels decided to take on the crown for independence,
they nominated George Washington to be "Commander of All
Continental Forces," at the Second Continental Congress in the summer
of 1775. He accepted the challenge to turn the ragged and inexperienced
group of men into a fighting force, but refused any pay. Three days
later, Washington wrote to his wife, Martha, about his appointment.*

My Dearest:

I am now set down to write to you on a subject which fills me with
inexpressible concern, and this concern is greatly aggravated and increased,
when I reflect upon the uneasiness I know it will give you. It has been
determined in Congress, that the whole army raised for the defense of the
American cause shall be put under my care, and that it is necessary for me to
proceed immediately to Boston to take upon me the command of it.

You may believe me, my dear Patsy, when I assure you, in the most solemn
manner that, so far from seeking this appointment, I have used every endeavor
in my power to avoid it, not only from my unwillingness to part with you and the
family, but from consciousness of its being a trust too great for my capacity, and
that I should enjoy more real happiness in one month with you at home, than I

have the most distant prospect of finding abroad, if my stay were to be seven times seven years. But as it has been a kind of destiny, that has thrown me upon this service, I shall hope that my undertaking is designed to answer some good purpose. You might, and I suppose did perceive, from the tenor of my letters, that I was apprehensive I could not avoid this appointment, as I did not pretend to intimate when I should return. That was the case. It was utterly out of my power to refuse this appointment, without exposing my character to such censures, as would have reflected dishonor upon myself, and given pain to my friends. This, I am sure, could not, and ought not, to be pleasing to you, and must have lessened me considerably in my own esteem. I shall rely, therefore, confidently on that Providence, which has heretofore preserved and been bountiful to me, not doubting but that I shall return safe to you in the fall. I shall feel no pain from the toil or the danger of the campaign; my unhappiness will flow from the uneasiness I know you will feel from being left alone. I therefore beg, that you will summon your whole fortitude, and pass your time as agreeably as possible....

As life is always uncertain, and common prudence dictates to every man the necessity of settling his temporal concerns, while it is in his power, and while the mind is calm and undisturbed, I have, since I came to this place (for I had not the time to do it before I left home) got Colonel Pendleton to draft a will for me, by the directions I gave him, which will I now enclose. The provision made for you in case of my death will, I hope, be agreeable.

I shall add nothing more, as I have several letters to write, but to desire that you will remember me to your friends, and to assure you that I am with the most unfeigned regard, my dear Patsy, your affectionate, &c.

G. Washington

FROM

PAUL REVERE'S RIDE

Henry Wadsworth Longfellow, 1860 (set in 1775)

Listen, my children, and you shall hear
Of the midnight ride of Paul Revere,
On the eighteenth of April, in Seventy-five;
Hardly a man is now alive
Who remembers that famous day and year.

He said to his friend, "If the British march
By land or sea from the town to-night,
Hang a lantern aloft in the belfry arch
Of the North Church tower as a signal light,—
One, if by land, and two, if by sea;
And I on the opposite shore will be,
Ready to ride and spread the alarm
Through every Middlesex village and farm,
For the country folk to be up and to arm."

Then he said, "Good night!" and with muffled oar
Silently rowed to the Charlestown shore,
Just as the moon rose over the bay,
Where swinging wide at her moorings lay
The Somerset, British man-of-war;

A phantom ship, with each mast and spar
Across the moon like a prison bar,
And a huge black hulk, that was magnified
By its own reflection in the tide.

Meanwhile, his friend, through alley and street,
Wanders and watches with eager ears,
Till in the silence around him he hears
The muster of men at the barrack door,
The sound of arms, and the tramp of feet,
And the measured tread of the grenadiers,
Marching down to their boats on the shore.

Then he climbed the tower of the Old North Church,
By the wooden stairs, with stealthy tread,
To the belfry-chamber overhead,
And startled the pigeons from their perch
On the sombre rafters, that round him made
Masses and moving shapes of shade,—
By the trembling ladder, steep and tall,
To the highest window in the wall,
Where he paused to listen and look down
A moment on the roofs of the town,
And the moonlight flowing over all....

A MOMENT ONLY HE FEELS THE SPELL
OF THE PLACE AND THE HOUR, AND THE SECRET DREAD
OF THE LONELY BELFRY AND THE DEAD;
FOR SUDDENLY ALL HIS THOUGHTS ARE BENT
ON A SHADOWY SOMETHING FAR AWAY,
WHERE THE RIVER WIDENS TO MEET THE BAY,—
A LINE OF BLACK THAT BENDS AND FLOATS
ON THE RISING TIDE, LIKE A BRIDGE OF BOATS.

MEANWHILE, IMPATIENT TO MOUNT AND RIDE,
BOOTED AND SPURRED, WITH A HEAVY STRIDE
ON THE OPPOSITE SHORE WALKED PAUL REVERE.
NOW HE PATTED HIS HORSE'S SIDE,
NOW GAZED AT THE LANDSCAPE FAR AND NEAR,
THEN, IMPETUOUS, STAMPED THE EARTH,
AND TURNED AND TIGHTENED HIS SADDLE-GIRTH;
BUT MOSTLY HE WATCHED WITH EAGER SEARCH
THE BELFRY-TOWER OF THE OLD NORTH CHURCH,
AS IT ROSE ABOVE THE GRAVES ON THE HILL,
LONELY AND SPECTRAL AND SOMBRE AND STILL.
AND LO! AS HE LOOKS, ON THE BELFRY'S HEIGHT
A GLIMMER, AND THEN A GLEAM OF LIGHT!

* * *

You know the rest. In the books you have read,
How the British Regulars fired and fled,—
How the farmers gave them ball for ball,
From behind each fence and farm-yard wall,
Chasing the red-coats down the lane,
Then crossing the fields to emerge again
Under the trees at the turn of the road,
And only pausing to fire and load.

So through the night rode Paul Revere;
And so through the night went his cry of alarm
To every Middlesex village and farm,—
A cry of defiance and not of fear,
A voice in the darkness, a knock at the door,
And a word that shall echo forevermore!
For, borne on the night-wind of the Past,
Through all our history, to the last,
In the hour of darkness and peril and need,
The people will waken and listen to hear
The hurrying hoof-beats of that steed,
And the midnight message of Paul Revere.

ABIGAIL ADAMS
TO JOHN ADAMS

BRAINTREE, MASSACHUSETTS, MARCH 31, 1776

Abigail and John Adams wrote frequently while John was in Philadelphia attending the Continental Congress. Abigail often offered political advice to her husband, and informed him of the state of affairs in wartime Boston. In the letter excerpted here, she wrote to John Adams of her excitement at the prospect of independence.

I feel very differently at the approach of spring to which I did a month ago. We knew not then whether we could plant or sow with safety, whether when we had toiled we could reap the fruits of our own industry, whether we could rest in our own Cottages, or whether we should not be driven from the sea coasts to seek shelter in the wilderness, but now we feel as if we might sit under our own vine and eat the good of the land.

I feel a *gaieti de Coar* to which before I was a stranger. I think the Sun looks brighter, the Birds sing more melodiously, and Nature puts on a more cheerfull countenance. We feel a temporary peace, and the poor fugitives are returning to their deserted habitations.

Tho we felicitate ourselves, we sympathize with those who are trembling least the Lot of Boston should be theirs. But they cannot be in similar circumstances unless pusillanimity and cowardice should take possession of them. They have time and warning given them to see the Evil and shun it. —I long to hear that you have declared an independency—and by the way, in the new Code of Laws which I suppose it will be necessary for you to make, I desire you would Remember the Ladies, and be more generous and favourable to them than your ancestors. Do not put such unlimited power into the hands of the Husbands. Remember, all Men would be tyrants if they could. If particular care and attention is not paid to the Ladies, we are determined to foment a Rebellion, and will not hold ourselves bound by any Laws in which we have no voice, or Representation.

That your Sex are Naturally Tyrannical is Truth so thoroughly established as to admit no dispute, but such of you as wish to be happy willingly give up the harsh title of Master for the more tender and endearing one of Friend. Why, then, not put it out of the power of the vicious and the Lawless to use us with cruelty and indignity with impunity. Men of Sense in all Ages abhor those customs which treat us only as the vassals of your Sex. Regard us then as Beings placed by providence under your protection, and in imitation of the Supreem Being, make use of that power only for our happiness.

Abigail

Presidents

George Washington (no party affiliation), served 1789–1797

John Adams (Federalist), served 1797–1801

Thomas Jefferson (Democratic-Republican), served 1801–1809

James Madison (D-R), served 1809–1817

James Monroe (D-R), served 1817–1825

John Quincy Adams (D-R), served 1825–1829

Andrew Jackson (D), served 1829–1837

Martin Van Buren (D), served 1837–1841

William Henry Harrison (Whig), served March 1841–April 4,1841 (died of pneumonia in office)

John Tyler (Whig), served 1841–1845.

James Knox Polk (D), served 1845–1849

Zachary Taylor (Whig), served March 1849–July 9, 1850 (died of illness in office)

Millard Fillmore (Whig), served 1850–1853

Franklin Pierce (D), served 1853–1857

James Buchanan (D), served 1857–1861

Abraham Lincoln (R), served March 1861–April 15, 1865 (assassinated in office)

Andrew Johnson (National Union), served 1865–1869

Ulysses S. Grant (R), served 1869–1877

Rutherford B. Hayes (R), served 1877–1881

James A. Garfield (R), served March 1881–September 17, 1881 (assassinated in office)

Chester A. Arthur (R), served 1881–1885

Grover Cleveland (D), served 1885–1889

Benjamin Harrison (R), served 1889–1893

Grover Cleveland (D), served 1893–1897

William Mckinley (R), served March 1897–September 14, 1901 (assassinated in office)

Theodore Roosevelt (R), served 1901–1909

William H. Taft (R), served 1909–1913

Woodrow Wilson (D), served 1913–1921

Warren G. Harding (R), served March 1921–August 2, 1923 (died of a heart attack in office)

Calvin Coolidge (R), served 1923–1929

Herbert C. Hoover (R), served 1929–1933

Franklin D. Roosevelt (R), served March 1933–April 12, 1945 (died of a cerebral hemorrhage in office)

Harry S. Truman (D), served 1945–1953

Dwight David Eisenhower (R), served 1953–1961

John F. Kennedy (D), served January 1961–November 22, 1963 (assassinated in office)

Lyndon B. Johnson (D), served 1963–1969

Richard M. Nixon (R), served January 1969–August 9, 1974 (resigned)

Gerald R. Ford (R), served 1974–1977

James E. Carter (D), served 1977–1981

Ronald W. Reagan (R), served 1981–1989

George H.W. Bush (R), served 1989–1993

William J. Clinton (D), served 1993–2001

George W. Bush (R), served 2001–Present

Seven presidents served one-year terms under the Articles of Confederation before George Washington was the first president elected under the new Constitution. The seven: John Hanson (1781–1782), Elias Boudinot (1782–1783), Thomas Mifflin (1783–1784), Richard Henry Lee (1784–1785), Nathan Gorman (1785–1786), Arthur St. Clair (1786–1787), and Cyrus Griffin (1787–1788).

John Adams and his friend Thomas Jefferson died on the same day—July 4, 1826. Adams died first. His last words were, "Thomas Jefferson still survives."

Thomas Jefferson liked to answer the White House door himself—often in slippers.

James Buchanan was the only bachelor president.

Grover Cleveland was the only president to serve two non-consecutive terms.

In 1906, Teddy Roosevelt was the first president to receive a Nobel Peace Prize, for mediating a peace agreement between Russia and Japan. Woodrow Wilson was the second: he won in 1919 for creating the League of Nations.

At 6'4" and over 300 lbs, William Howard Taft was our biggest president.

Sheep grazed on Woodrow Wilson's White House lawn during WW I. Their wool was sold to profit the Red Cross.

FDR was the only president elected to three terms.

JFK was America's first Catholic president.

Gerald Ford and his wife, Betty, worked as models before they married.

Jimmy Carter was the first American president born in a hospital.

The Declaration of Independence

IN CONGRESS, JULY 4, 1776

When in the Course of human events it becomes necessary for one people to dissolve the political bands which have connected them with another, and to assume among the powers of the earth, the separate and equal station to which the Laws of Nature and of Nature's God entitle them, a decent respect to the opinions of mankind requires that they should declare the causes which impel them to the separation.

We hold these truths to be self-evident, that all men are created equal, that they are endowed by their Creator with certain unalienable Rights, that among these are Life, Liberty and the pursuit of Happiness. That to secure these rights, Governments are instituted among Men, deriving their just powers from the consent of the governed, That whenever any Form of Government becomes destructive of these ends, it is the Right of the People to alter or to abolish it, and to institute new Government, laying its foundation on such principles and organizing its powers in such form, as to them shall seem most likely to effect their Safety and Happiness....

THOMAS JEFFERSON
TO JAMES MADISON
PARIS, DECEMBER 20, 1787

*Thomas Jefferson was in Paris during the Continental Congress,
but received a draft of the document and report of the goings-on
from friend James Madison. Jefferson's response, excerpted here,
includes a persuasive argument for a bill of rights.*

I like much the general idea of framing a government, which
should go on of itself, peaceably, without needing continual recur-
rence to the State legislatures. I like the organization of the
government into legislative, judiciary and executive. I like the
power given the legislature to levy taxes, and for that reason solely,
I approve of the greater House being chosen by the people
directly....I am captivated by the compromise of the opposite
claims of the great and little States, of the latter to equal, and the
former to proportional influence. I am much pleased too, with the
substitution of the method of voting by person, instead of that of
voting by States; and I like the negative given to the Executive,
conjointly with a third of either House....

I will now tell you what I do not like. First, the omission of a bill of rights, providing clearly, and without the aid of sophism, for freedom of religion, freedom of the press, protection against standing armies, restriction of monopolies, the eternal and unremitting force of the habeas corpus laws, and trials by jury in all matters of fact triable by the laws of the land, and not by the laws of nations....I have a right to nothing, which another has a right to take away; and Congress will have a right to take away trials by jury in all civil cases. Let me add, that a bill of rights is what the people are entitled to against every government on earth, general or particular, and what no just government should refuse, or rest on inference....

At all events, I hope you will not be discouraged from making other trials, if the present one should fail. We are never permitted to despair of the commonwealth. I have thus told you freely what I like, and what I dislike, merely as a matter of curiosity; for I know it is not in my power to offer matter of information to your judgment, which has been formed after hearing and weighing everything which the wisdom of man could offer on these subjects. I own, I am not a friend to a very energetic government. It is always oppressive. It places the governors

indeed more at their ease, at the expense of the people. The late rebellion in Massachusetts has given more alarm, than I think it should have done. Calculate that one rebellion in thirteen States in the course of eleven years, is but one for each State in a century and a half. No country should be so long without one. Nor will any degree of power in the hands of government, prevent insurrections....Educate and inform the whole mass of the people. Enable them to see that it is their interest to preserve peace and order, and they will preserve them. And it requires no very high degree of education to convince them of this. They are the only sure reliance for the preservation of our liberty. After all, it is my principle that the will of the majority should prevail. If they approve the proposed constitution in all its parts, I shall concur in it cheerfully, in hopes they will amend it, whenever they shall find it works wrong. This reliance cannot deceive us, as long as we remain virtuous; and I think we shall be so, as long as agriculture is our principal object, which will be the case, while there remains vacant lands in any part of America. When we get piled upon one another in large cities, as in Europe, we shall become corrupt as in Europe, and go to eating one another as they do there....

Th: Jefferson

The Preamble to the Bill of Rights

NEW YORK, 1789

CONGRESS OF THE UNITED STATES
begun and held at the City of New-York, on
Wednesday the fourth of March, one thousand seven hundred
and eighty nine.

THE Conventions of a number of the States, having at the time of
their adopting the Constitution, expressed a desire, in order to prevent
misconstruction or abuse of its powers, that further declaratory and
restrictive clauses should be added: And as extending the ground of
public confidence in the Government, will best ensure the beneficent
ends of its institution.

RESOLVED by the Senate and House of Representatives of the United
States of America, in Congress assembled, two thirds of both Houses
concurring, that the following Articles be proposed to the Legislatures
of the several States, as amendments to the Constitution of the United
States, all, or any of which Articles, when ratified by three fourths of

the said Legislatures, to be valid to all intents and purposes, as part of the said Constitution; viz.

ARTICLES in addition to, and Amendment of the Constitution of the United States of America, proposed by Congress, and ratified by the Legislatures of the several States, pursuant to the fifth Article of the original Constitution.

AMENDMENT I
Congress shall make no law respecting an establishment of religion, or prohibiting the free exercise thereof; or abridging the freedom of speech, or of the press; or the right of the people peaceably to assemble, and to petition the Government for a redress of grievances.

AMENDMENT II
A well regulated Militia, being necessary to the security of a free State, the right of the people to keep and bear Arms, shall not be infringed.

AMENDMENT III
No Soldier shall, in time of peace be quartered in any house, without the consent of the Owner, nor in time of war, but in a manner to be prescribed by law.

AMENDMENT IV
The right of the people to be secure in their persons, houses, papers, and effects, against unreasonable searches and seizures, shall not be violated, and no Warrants shall issue, but upon probable cause,

supported by Oath or affirmation, and particularly describing the place
to be searched, and the persons or things to be seized.

AMENDMENT V

No person shall be held to answer for a capital, or otherwise infamous
crime, unless on a presentment or indictment of a Grand Jury, except
in cases arising in the land or naval forces, or in the Militia, when in
actual service in time of War or public danger; nor shall any person be
subject for the same offence to be twice put in jeopardy of life or limb;
nor shall be compelled in any criminal case to be a witness against
himself, nor be deprived of life, liberty, or property, without due process
of law; nor shall private property be taken for public use, without just
compensation.

AMENDMENT VI

In all criminal prosecutions, the accused shall enjoy the right to a
speedy and public trial, by an impartial jury of the State and district
wherein the crime shall have been committed, which district shall have
been previously ascertained by law, and to be informed of the nature
and cause of the accusation; to be confronted with the witnesses against
him; to have compulsory process for obtaining witnesses in his favor,
and to have the Assistance of Counsel for his defense.

AMENDMENT VII

In suits at common law, where the value in controversy shall exceed
twenty dollars, the right of trial by jury shall be preserved, and no fact

tried by a jury, shall be otherwise reexamined in any Court of the
United States, than according to the rules of the common law.

AMENDMENT VIII
Excessive bail shall not be required, nor excessive fines imposed,
nor cruel and unusual punishments inflicted.

AMENDMENT IX
The enumeration in the Constitution, of certain rights, shall not
be construed to deny or disparage others retained by the people.

AMENDMENT X
The powers not delegated to the United States by the Constitution,
nor prohibited by it to the States, are reserved to the States
respectively, or to the people.

AMENDMENT XI
Passed by Congress March 4, 1794. Ratified February 7, 1795.
The Judicial power of the United States shall not be construed to extend
to any suit in law or equity, commenced or prosecuted against one of
the United States by Citizens of another State, or by Citizens or
Subjects of any Foreign State.

AMENDMENT XII
Passed by Congress December 9, 1803. Ratified June 15, 1804.
The Electors shall meet in their respective states and vote by ballot for
President and Vice-President, one of whom, at least, shall not be an

inhabitant of the same state with themselves; they shall name in their ballots the person voted for as President, and in distinct ballots the person voted for as Vice-President, and they shall make distinct lists of all persons voted for as President, and of all persons voted for as Vice-President, and of the number of votes for each, which lists they shall sign and certify, and transmit sealed to the seat of the government of the United States, directed to the President of the Senate;—the President of the Senate shall, in the presence of the Senate and House of Representatives, open all the certificates and the votes shall then be counted;—The person having the greatest number of votes for President, shall be the President, if such number be a majority of the whole number of Electors appointed; and if no person have such majority, then from the persons having the highest numbers not exceeding three on the list of those voted for as President, the House of Representatives shall choose immediately, by ballot, the President. But in choosing the President, the votes shall be taken by states, the representation from each state having one vote; a quorum for this purpose shall consist of a member or members from two-thirds of the states, and a majority of all the states shall be necessary to a choice. [And if the House of Representatives shall not choose a President whenever the right of choice shall devolve upon them, before the fourth day of March next following, then the Vice-President shall act as President, as in case of the death or other constitutional disability of the President.—]* The person having the greatest number of votes as Vice-President, shall be the Vice-President, if such number be a majority of the whole number of Electors appointed, and if no person have a majority, then from the two highest numbers on the list, the Senate shall choose the Vice-President; a quorum for the purpose shall consist of two-thirds of the whole number of Senators, and a majority of the whole number shall be necessary to a choice. But no person constitutionally ineligible to the office of President shall be eligible to that of Vice-President of the United States. *Superseded by section 3 of the 20th amendment.*

AMENDMENT XIII
Passed by Congress January 31, 1865. Ratified December 6, 1865.

SECTION 1.
Neither slavery nor involuntary servitude, except as a punishment for crime whereof the party shall have been duly convicted, shall exist within the United States, or any place subject to their jurisdiction.

SECTION 2.
Congress shall have power to enforce this article by appropriate legislation.

AMENDMENT XIV
Passed by Congress June 13, 1866. Ratified July 9, 1868.

SECTION 1.
All persons born or naturalized in the United States, and subject to the jurisdiction thereof, are citizens of the United States and of the State wherein they reside. No State shall make or enforce any law which

shall abridge the privileges or immunities of citizens of the United States; nor shall any State deprive any person of life, liberty, or property, without due process of law; nor deny to any person within its jurisdiction the equal protection of the laws.

SECTION 2.

Representatives shall be apportioned among the several States according to their respective numbers, counting the whole number of persons in each State, excluding Indians not taxed. But when the right to vote at any election for the choice of electors for President and Vice-President of the United States, Representatives in Congress, the Executive and Judicial officers of a State, or the members of the Legislature thereof, is denied to any of the male inhabitants of such State, being twenty-one years of age, and citizens of the United States, or in any way abridged, except for participation in rebellion, or other crime, the basis of representation therein shall be reduced in the proportion which the number of such male citizens shall bear to the whole number of male citizens twenty-one years of age in such State.

SECTION 3.

No person shall be a Senator or Representative in Congress, or elector of President and Vice-President, or hold any office, civil or military, under the United States, or under any State, who, having previously taken an oath, as a member of Congress, or as an officer of the United States, or as a member of any State legislature, or as an executive or judicial officer of any State, to support the Constitution of the United States, shall have engaged in insurrection or rebellion against the same, or given aid or comfort to the enemies thereof. But Congress may by a vote of two-thirds of each House, remove such disability.

SECTION 4.

The validity of the public debt of the United States, authorized by law, including debts incurred for payment of pensions and bounties for services in suppressing insurrection or rebellion, shall not be questioned. But neither the United States nor any State shall assume or pay any debt or obligation incurred in aid of insurrection or rebellion against the United States, or any claim for the loss or emancipation of any slave; but all such debts, obligations and claims shall be held illegal and void.

SECTION 5.

The Congress shall have the power to enforce, by appropriate legislation, the provisions of this article.

AMENDMENT XV

Passed by Congress February 26, 1869. Ratified February 3, 1870.

Section 1.

The right of citizens of the United States to vote shall not be denied or abridged by the United States or by any State on account of race, color, or previous condition of servitude—

Section 2.

The Congress shall have the power to enforce this article by appropriate legislation.

Amendment XVI

Passed by Congress July 2, 1909. Ratified February 3, 1913.

The Congress shall have power to lay and collect taxes on incomes, from whatever source derived, without apportionment among the several States, and without regard to any census or enumeration.

Amendment XVII

Passed by Congress May 13, 1912. Ratified April 8, 1913.

The Senate of the United States shall be composed of two Senators from each State, elected by the people thereof, for six years; and each Senator shall have one vote. The electors in each State shall have the qualifications requisite for electors of the most numerous branch of the State legislatures.

When vacancies happen in the representation of any State in the Senate, the executive authority of such State shall issue writs of election to fill such vacancies: *Provided*, That the legislature of any State may empower the executive thereof to make temporary appointments until the people fill the vacancies by election as the legislature may direct.

This amendment shall not be so construed as to affect the election or term of any Senator chosen before it becomes valid as part of the Constitution.

AMENDMENT XVIII
Passed by Congress December 18, 1917. Ratified January 16, 1919. Repealed by amendment 21.

SECTION 1.
After one year from the ratification of this article the manufacture, sale, or transportation of intoxicating liquors within, the importation thereof into, or the exportation thereof from the United States and all territory subject to the jurisdiction thereof for beverage purposes is hereby prohibited.

SECTION 2.
The Congress and the several States shall have concurrent power to enforce this article by appropriate legislation.

SECTION 3.
This article shall be inoperative unless it shall have been ratified as an amendment to the Constitution by the legislatures of the several States, as provided in the Constitution, within seven years from the date of the submission hereof to the States by the Congress.

AMENDMENT XIX

Passed by Congress June 4, 1919. Ratified August 18, 1920.

The right of citizens of the United States to vote shall not be denied or abridged by the United States or by any State on account of sex.

Congress shall have power to enforce this article by appropriate legislation.

AMENDMENT XX

Passed by Congress March 2, 1932. Ratified January 23, 1933.

SECTION 1.

The terms of the President and the Vice President shall end at noon on the 20th day of January, and the terms of Senators and Representatives at noon on the 3d day of January, of the years in which such terms would have ended if this article had not been ratified; and the terms of their successors shall then begin.

SECTION 2.

The Congress shall assemble at least once in every year, and such meeting shall begin at noon on the 3d day of January, unless they shall by law appoint a different day.

SECTION 3.

If, at the time fixed for the beginning of the term of the President, the President elect shall have died, the Vice President elect shall become President. If a President shall not have been chosen before the time

fixed for the beginning of his term, or if the President elect shall have failed to qualify, then the Vice President elect shall act as President until a President shall have qualified; and the Congress may by law provide for the case wherein neither a President elect nor a Vice President shall have qualified, declaring who shall then act as President, or the manner in which one who is to act shall be selected, and such person shall act accordingly until a President or Vice President shall have qualified.

SECTION 4.
The Congress may by law provide for the case of the death of any of the persons from whom the House of Representatives may choose a President whenever the right of choice shall have devolved upon them, and for the case of the death of any of the persons from whom the Senate may choose a Vice President whenever the right of choice shall have devolved upon them.

SECTION 5.
Sections 1 and 2 shall take effect on the 15th day of October following the ratification of this article.

SECTION 6.
This article shall be inoperative unless it shall have been ratified as an amendment to the Constitution by the legislatures of three-fourths of the several States within seven years from the date of its submission.

Amendment XXI

Passed by Congress February 20, 1933. Ratified December 5, 1933.

Section 1.

The eighteenth article of amendment to the Constitution of the United States is hereby repealed.

Section 2.

The transportation or importation into any State, Territory, or Possession of the United States for delivery or use therein of intoxicating liquors, in violation of the laws thereof, is hereby prohibited.

Section 3.

This article shall be inoperative unless it shall have been ratified as an amendment to the Constitution by conventions in the several States, as provided in the Constitution, within seven years from the date of the submission hereof to the States by the Congress.

Amendment XXII

Passed by Congress March 21, 1947. Ratified February 27, 1951.

Section 1.

No person shall be elected to the office of the President more than twice, and no person who has held the office of President, or acted as President, for more than two years of a term to which some other person was elected President shall be elected to the office of President more than once. But this Article shall not apply to any person holding the office of President when this Article was proposed by Congress, and shall not prevent any person who may be holding the office of President, or acting as President, during the term within which this Article becomes operative from holding the office of President or acting as President during the remainder of such term.

Section 2.

This article shall be inoperative unless it shall have been ratified as an amendment to the Constitution by the legislatures of three-fourths of the several States within seven years from the date of its submission to the States by the Congress.

Amendment XXIII

Passed by Congress June 16, 1960. Ratified March 29, 1961.

Section 1.

The District constituting the seat of Government of the United States shall appoint in such manner as Congress may direct:

A number of electors of President and Vice President equal to the whole number of Senators and Representatives in Congress to which the District would be entitled if it were a State, but in no event more than the least populous State; they shall be in addition to those appointed by the States, but they shall be considered, for the purposes of the election of President and Vice President, to be electors appointed by a State; and they shall meet in the District and perform such duties as provided by the twelfth article of amendment.

SECTION 2.

The Congress shall have power to enforce this article by appropriate legislation.

AMENDMENT XXIV
Passed by Congress August 27, 1962. Ratified January 23, 1964.

SECTION 1.

The right of citizens of the United States to vote in any primary or other election for President or Vice President, for electors for President or Vice President, or for Senator or Representative in Congress, shall not be denied or abridged by the United States or any State by reason of failure to pay poll tax or other tax.

SECTION 2.

The Congress shall have power to enforce this article by appropriate legislation.

AMENDMENT XXV
Passed by Congress July 6, 1965. Ratified February 10, 1967.

SECTION 1.

In case of the removal of the President from office or of his death or resignation, the Vice President shall become President.

SECTION 2.

Whenever there is a vacancy in the office of the Vice President, the President shall nominate a Vice President who shall take office upon confirmation by a majority vote of both Houses of Congress.

Section 3.

Whenever the President transmits to the President pro tempore of the Senate and the Speaker of the House of Representatives his written declaration that he is unable to discharge the powers and duties of his office, and until he transmits to them a written declaration to the contrary, such powers and duties shall be discharged by the Vice President as Acting President.

Section 4.

Whenever the Vice President and a majority of either the principal officers of the executive departments or of such other body as Congress may by law provide, transmit to the President pro tempore of the Senate and the Speaker of the House of Representatives their written declaration that the President is unable to discharge the powers and duties of his office, the Vice President shall immediately assume the powers and duties of the office as Acting President.

Thereafter, when the President transmits to the President pro tempore of the Senate and the Speaker of the House of Representatives his written declaration that no inability exists, he shall resume the powers and duties of his office unless the Vice President and a majority of either the principal officers of the executive department or of such other body as Congress may by law provide, transmit within four days to the President pro tempore of the Senate and the Speaker of the House of Representatives their written declaration that the President is unable to discharge the powers and duties of his office. Thereupon Congress shall decide the issue, assembling within forty-eight hours for that purpose if not in session. If the Congress, within twenty-one days after receipt of the latter written declaration, or, if Congress is not in session, within twenty-one days after Congress is required to assemble, determines by two-thirds vote of both Houses that the President is unable to discharge the powers and duties of his office, the Vice President shall continue to discharge the same as Acting President; otherwise, the President shall resume the powers and duties of his office.

Amendment XXVI
Passed by Congress March 23, 1971. Ratified July 1, 1971.

Section 1.
The right of citizens of the United States, who are eighteen years of age or older, to vote shall not be denied or abridged by the United States or by any State on account of age.

Section 2.
The Congress shall have power to enforce this article by appropriate legislation.

Amendment XXVII
Originally proposed Sept. 25, 1789. Ratified May 7, 1992.

No law, varying the compensation for the services of the Senators and Representatives, shall take effect, until an election of representatives shall have intervened.

William Cobbett
to Miss Rachel Smithers

Philadelphia, July 6, 1794

Like many English, William Cobbett arrived in America in 1792 with high hopes. In an excerpt from his letter to friend Rachel Smithers back in England, he expressed his disappointment.

This country is good for getting money, that is to say, if a person is industrious and enterprising. In every other respect the country is miserable. Exactly the contrary of what I expected. The land is bad, rocky; houses wretched; roads impassable after the least rain. Fruit in quantity, but good for nothing. One apple or peach in England or France is worth a bushel of them here. The seasons are detestable. All is burning or freezing. There is no spring or autumn. The weather is so very inconstant that you are never sure for an hour, a single hour at a time. Last night we made a fire to sit by, and to-day it is scorching hot. The whole month of March was so hot that we could hardly bear our clothes, and three parts of the month of June there was frost every night, and so cold in the

day-time that we were obliged to wear great-coats. The people are worthy of the country—cheating, sly, roguish gang. Strangers make fortunes here in spite of all this, particularly the English. The natives are by nature idle, and seek to live by cheating, while foreigners, being industrious, seek no other means than those dictated by integrity, and are sure to meet with encouragement even from the idle and roguish themselves; for, however roguish a man may be, he always loves to deal with an honest man. You have perhaps heard of the plague being at Philadelphia last year. It was no plague; it was a fever of the country, and is by no means extra-ordinary among the Americans. In the fall of the year almost every person, in every place, has a spell of fever that is called fall-fever. It is often fatal, and the only way to avoid it is to quit the country. But this fever is not all. Every month has its particular malady. In July, for example, everybody almost, or at least one half of the people, are taken with vomitings for several days at a time; they often carry off the patient, and almost always children. In short, the country is altogether detestable....

Wm. Cobbett

THE STAR-SPANGLED BANNER

Francis Scott Key, 1814

Oh, say can you see by the dawn's early light
What so proudly we hail'd at the twilight's last gleaming,
Whose broad stripes and bright stars through the perilous fight,
O'er the ramparts we watch'd, were so gallantly streaming?
And the rockets' red glare, the bombs bursting in air,
Gave proof through the night that our flag was still there.
Oh say does that star-spangled banner yet wave
O'er the land of the free and the home of the brave?

On the shore dimly seen through the mists of the deep,
Where the foe's haughty host in dread silence reposes,
What is that which the breeze, o'er the towering steep,
As it fitfully blows, half conceals, half discloses?
Now it catches the gleam of the morning's first beam,
In full glory reflected now shines on the stream:
'Tis the star-spangled banner, oh, long may it wave
O'er the land of the free and the home of the brave!

And where is that band who so vauntingly swore
That the havoc of war and the battle's confusion
A home and a country should leave us no more?
Their blood has wash'd out their foul footstep's pollution.
No refuge could save the hireling and slave
From the terror of flight or the gloom of the grave,
And the star-spangled banner in triumph doth wave
O'er the land of the free and the home of the brave.

Oh, thus be it ever, when freemen shall stand
Between their lov'd home and the war's desolation!
Blest with vict'ry and peace may the heav'n-rescued land
Praise the Power that hath made and preserv'd us a nation!
Then conquer we must, when our cause it is just,
And this be our motto, "In God is our trust."
And the star-spangled banner in triumph wave
O'er the land of the free and the home of the brave!

67

Vegetable Sides

These are all great Southern dishes, very healthy and delicious. A little Tabasco won't hurt, either. They are great with barbecued ribs or chicken.

Collard Greens

10 ounces bacon

4 pounds collard greens, stalks removed

1 tablespoon sugar

2 tablespoons cider vinegar

Pickapeppa sauce

salt and freshly milled pepper

1. Fry the bacon, and then add collard greens and 6 quarts of water. Simmer for two hours.

2. Add sugar, cider vinegar, Pickapeppa sauce and salt and pepper. Mix and then drain. Serve.

Serves 6 to 8.

Black-Eyed Peas

2 ¹/₂ cups dry black-eyed peas

¹/₂ pound fresh pork fat-back, cut into 1″ cubes

6 small yellow onions, peeled

salt and pepper to taste

1. Place the peas and onions in a large pot and add at least 2 quarts of water.

2. Bring to a boil, turn off the heat and let stand for an hour. Add the pork and simmer for two hours, or until peas are tender. Add more water if needed to keep everything soupy.

3. Salt and pepper to taste. Serve.

Serves 6 to 8.

Old Ironsides

Oliver Wendell Holmes, 1830

Ay, tear her tattered ensign down!
   Long has it waved on high,
And many an eye has danced to see
   That banner in the sky;
Beneath it rung the battle shout,
   And burst the cannon's roar;—
The meteor of the ocean air
   Shall sweep the clouds no more.

Her deck, once red with heroes' blood,
   Where knelt the vanquished foe,
When winds were hurrying o'er the flood,
And waves were white below,

No more shall feel the victor's tread,
    Or know the conquered knee;—
The harpies of the shore shall pluck
    The eagle of the sea!

Oh better that her shattered hulk
    Should sink beneath the wave;
Her thunders shook the mighty deep,
    And there should be her grave;
Nail to the mast her holy flag,
    Set every threadbare sail,
And give her to the god of storms,
    The lightning and the gale!

AMERICA

SAMUEL FRANCIS SMITH, 1831

My country, 'tis of thee,
Sweet land of liberty,
Of thee I sing;
Land where my fathers died,
Land of the Pilgrim's pride,
From ev'ry mountainside
Let freedom ring!

My native country, thee,
Land of the noble free,
Thy name I love;
I love thy rocks and rills,
Thy woods and templed hills;
My heart with rapture thrills,
Like that above.

Let music swell the breeze,
And ring from all the trees
Sweet freedom's song.
Let mortal tongues awake;
Let all that breathe partake;
Let rocks their silence break,
The sound prolong.

Our father's God, to Thee,
Author of liberty,
To Thee we sing.
Long may our land be bright
With freedom's holy light;
Protect us by Thy might,
Great God, our King!

ADDRESS TO THE BRITISH PEOPLE

FREDERICK DOUGLASS, MAY 12, 1846

A self-educated slave who escaped in 1838 and headed North, Frederick Douglass became a renowned orator against slavery and was soon traced by his former owner. In the early 1840s he went on a speaking tour of England to raise the funds to buy his freedom.

I DENY THE CHARGE that I am saying a word against the institutions of America, or the people, as such. What I have to say is against slavery and slaveholders. I feel at liberty to speak on this subject. I have on my back the marks of the lash; I have four sisters and one brother now under the galling chain. I feel it my duty to cry aloud and spare not. I am not averse to having the good opinion of my fellow-creatures. I am not averse to being kindly regarded by all men; but I am bound, even at the hazard of making a large class of religionists in this country hate me, oppose me, and malign me as they have done—I am bound by the prayers, and tears, and entreaties of three millions of kneeling bondsmen, to have no compromise with men who are in any shape or form connected with the slaveholders of America. I expose slavery in this country, because to expose it is to kill it. Slavery is one of those monsters of darkness to whom the light of truth is death. Expose slavery, and it dies. Light is to slavery what the heat of the sun is to the root of a tree; it must die under it....The slaveholders want total darkness on the subject. They want the hatchway shut down, that the monster may crawl in his den of darkness, crushing human hopes and happiness, destroying the bondman at will, and having no one to reprove or rebuke him. Slavery shrinks from the light; it hateth the light, neither cometh to the light, lest its deeds should be reproved. To tear off the mask from this abominable system, to expose it to the light of heaven, aye, to the heat of the sun, that it may burn and wither it out of existence, is my object in coming to this country. I want the slaveholder surrounded, as by a wall of anti-slavery fire, so that he may see the condemnation of himself and his system glaring down in letters of light. I want him to feel that he has no sympathy in England, Scotland, or Ireland; that he has none in Canada, none in Mexico, none among the poor wild Indians; that the voice of the civilized, aye, and savage world is against him. I would have condemnation blaze down upon him in every direction, till, stunned and overwhelmed with shame and confusion, he is compelled to let go the grasp he holds upon the persons of his victims, and restore them to their long-lost rights.

New England

✳

Nuclear Submarines are refitted in Portsmouth, New Hampshire.

✳

New Hampshire resident Levi Hutchins invented the world's first alarm clock in 1787. It was designed to ring only at 4AM.

✳

Maine has 60 lighthouses, including the Portland Head Light, commissioned by George Washington.

✳

Approximately one-third of Maine's population is of French, French-Canadian, or Acadian ancestry; 7% of Maine's population speak French at home.

✳

There are roughly 25,000 moose wandering around Maine.

✳

The tradition of Christmas Eve caroling reputedly began in Boston, Massachusetts, in the late 1800s.

✳

Vermont has the highest ratio of dairy cows to humans—about one cow for every four people (Wisconsin has the largest number of dairy cows, at 1,410,000).

✳

Vermont's skiers log 4 million ski days a year.

The ubiquitous yellow smiley face was invented by commercial illustrator Harvey Ball in Worcester, Massachusetts. He dreamt up the symbol in 1963 for an insurance company's morale-boosting campaign.

In 1957, 265 years after the last "witches" were hung in Salem Village in 1692, the state of Massachusetts issued a formal apology, officially clearing the names of many who had been accused.

Basketball coach William George Morgan invented the sport of mintonette in Holyoke, Massachusetts in 1895. He later renamed it volleyball.

⋆

The praying mantis is the official state insect of Connecticut.

The oldest synagogue in North America is Newport, Rhode Island's Touro Synagogue, founded in 1763.

Massachusetts passed the nation's first law against smoking in public in 1632. The concern was a moral one, however, and had nothing to do with health.

The original Thanksgiving feast could have included cranberry sauce— Massachusetts yields the country's biggest cranberry crop. (The official state beverage is cranberry juice, too.)

Rhode Island's motto is simply: "Hope."

America's first hamburger was served at Louie's Lunch in New Haven, Connecticut in 1895.

NANTUCKET

Nothing more happened on the passage worthy the mentioning; so, after a fine run, we safely arrived in Nantucket.

Nantucket! Take out your map and look at it. See what a real corner of the world it occupies; how it stands there, away off shore, more lonely than the Eddystone lighthouse. Look at it—a mere hillock, and elbow of sand; all beach, without a background. There is more sand there than you would use in twenty years as a substitute for blotting paper. Some gamesome wights will tell you that they have to plant weeds there, they don't grow naturally; that they import Canada thistles; that they have to send beyond seas for a spile to stop a leak in an oil cask; that pieces of wood in Nantucket are carried about like bits of the true cross in Rome; that people there plant toadstools before their houses, to get under the shade in summer time; that one blade of grass makes an oasis, three blades in a day's walk a prairie; that they wear quicksand shoes, something

like Laplander snowshoes; that they are so shut up, belted about, every way inclosed, surrounded, and made an utter island of by the ocean, that to their very chairs and tables small clams will sometimes be found adhering, as to the backs of sea turtles. But these extravaganzas only show that Nantucket is no Illinois.

Look now at the wondrous traditional story of how this island was settled by the red-men. Thus goes the legend. In olden times an eagle swooped down upon the New England coast, and carried off an infant Indian in his talons. With loud lament the parents saw their child borne out of sight over the wide waters. They resolved to follow the same direction. Setting out in their canoes, after a perilous passage they discovered the island, and there they found an empty ivory casket,— the poor little Indian's skeleton.

What wonder then, that these Nantucketers, born on a beach, should take

MOBY DICK

to the sea for a livelihood! They first caught crabs and quahogs in the sand; grown bolder, they waded out with nets for mackerel; more experienced, they pushed off in boats and captured cod; and at last, launching a navy of great ships on the sea, explored this watery world; put an incessant belt of circumnavigations round it; peeped in at Behring's Straights; and in all seasons and all oceans declared everlasting war with the mightiest animated mass that has survived the flood; most monstrous and most mountainous! That Himmalehan, salt-sea Mastodon, clothed with such portentousness of unconscious power, that his very panics are more to be dreaded than his most fearless and malicious assaults!

And thus have these naked Nantucketers, these sea hermits, issuing from their ant-hill in the sea, overrun and conquered the watery world like so many Alexanders; parcelling out among them the Atlantic, Pacific, and Indian oceans, as the three pirate powers did Poland. Let America add Mexico to Texas, and pile Cuba upon Canada; let the English overswarm all India, and hang out their blazing banner from the sun; two thirds of this terraqueous globe are the Nantucketer's. For the sea is his; he owns it, as Emperors

MOBY DICK

own empires; other seamen having but a right of way through it. Merchant ships are but extension bridges; armed ones but floating forts; even pirates and privateers, though following the sea as highwaymen the road, they but plunder other ships, other fragments of the land like themselves, without seeking to draw their living from the bottomless deep itself. The Nantucketer, he alone resides and riots on the sea; he alone, in Bible language, goes down to it in ships; to and fro ploughing it as his own special plantation. *There* is his home; *there* lies his business which a Noah's flood would not interrupt, though it overwhelmed all the millions in China. He lives on the sea, as prairie cocks in the prairie; he hides among the waves, he climbs them as chamois hunters climb the Alps. For years he knows not the land; so that when he comes to it at last, it smells like another world, more strangely than the moon would to an Earthsman. With the landless gull, that at sunset folds her wings and is rocked to sleep between billows; so at nightfall, the Nantucketer, out of sight of land, furls his sails, and lays him to his rest, while under his very pillow rush herds of walruses and whales.

New England Clam Chowder

There is another version of this chowder, made with a tomato base instead of cream, which goes by the name Manhattan Clam Chowder. The very notion of such a variation is considered a crime in the state of Maine, where they once tried to pass a law against it. Here is the classic recipe.

4 tablespoons butter

2 medium yellow onions, peeled and diced

2 tablespoons white flour

4 cups chicken stock

3 russet potatoes, peeled and diced

4 carrots, peeled and finely diced

1 cup leeks, diced

2 teaspoons fresh thyme leaves

1/4 cup chopped fresh parsley

4 cups shucked cherrystone clams, quartered

2 cups clam juice

1/2 cup half-and-half

1. Heat the butter in a large, heavy pot and sauté the onions over medium-low heat until translucent, about 10 minutes. Sprinkle flour over the onions and cook for another couple of minutes.

2. Add chicken stock slowly, blending as you go, then add the potatoes, carrots, leeks and herbs. Simmer another 10 minutes.

3. Add the clams and the clam juice, reduce heat to low, cover the pot, and slowly simmer until the potatoes are fork tender (another 15 minutes). Add half-and-half and cook another 5 minutes. Serve with oyster crackers.

Serves 8.

LOBSTER ROLLS

This quintessential New England meal actually originated in Connecticut. You have to serve them on hot dog buns to be authentic. They're perfect on a hot summer afternoon with a tall glass of lemonade, or on a cool evening accompanied by a cup of New England Clam Chowder

3 tablespoons mayonnaise

1 teaspoon Dijon mustard

2 teaspoons diced scallions

2 tablespoons lemon juice

salt and pepper to taste

cooked and chilled lobster meat from two 1 pound lobsters, cut into small chunks

$1/2$ cup chopped lettuce (I like iceberg or romaine)

2 celery ribs, finely chopped

4 buttered hot dog rolls

1. Mix mayonnaise, mustard, scallions, lemon juice, salt, and pepper. Then add lobster meat, chopped lettuce, and celery.

2. Place open buttered rolls face down in a hot skillet for about one minute to toast.

3. Fill the hot dog rolls, and feast.

Serves 4.

"IF YOU HAVE WOMAN'S RIGHTS, GIVE THEM TO HER"

SOJOURNER TRUTH, AKRON, OHIO, MAY 29, 1851

Sojourner Truth was born a slave in New York in 1797. Thirty-one years later she was freed, changed her name from Isabella, and began traveling the country speaking out against slavery and for women's rights. She gave this speech at the 1851 Ohio Woman's Rights Convention.

I AM a woman's rights.

I have as much muscle as any man, and can do as much work as any man. I have plowed and reaped and husked and chopped and mowed, and can any man do more than that?…

I have heard much about the sexes being equal….As for intellect all I can say is, if a woman [has] a pint and man a quart—why can't she have her little pint full? You need not be afraid to give us our rights for fear we will take too much, for we can't take more than our pint'll hold.

The poor men seem to be all in confusion, and don't know what to do. Why children, if you have woman's rights, give [them] to her and you will feel better. You will have your own rights, and they won't be so much trouble.

I can't read, but I can hear. I have heard the Bible and have learned that Eve caused man to sin. Well, if woman upset the world, do give her a chance to set it right side up again. The lady has spoken about Jesus, how he never spurned woman from him, and she was right….And how came Jesus into the world? Through God who created him and woman who bore him. Man, where is your part?…

But man is in a tight place, the poor slave is on him, woman is coming on him, and he is surely between a hawk and a buzzard.

FROM

LEAVES OF GRASS

WALT WHITMAN, 1855

I AM OF OLD AND YOUNG, OF THE FOOLISH AS MUCH AS THE WISE,

REGARDLESS OF OTHERS, EVER REGARDFUL OF OTHERS,

MATERNAL AS WELL AS PATERNAL, A CHILD AS WELL AS A MAN,

STUFF'D WITH THE STUFF THAT IS COARSE AND STUFF'D WITH THE STUFF THAT IS FINE,

ONE OF THE NATION OF MANY NATIONS, THE SMALLEST THE SAME
    AND THE LARGEST THE SAME,

A SOUTHERNER SOON AS A NORTHERNER, A PLANTER NONCHALANT AND HOSPITABLE
    DOWN BY THE OCONEE I LIVE,

A YANKEE BOUND MY OWN WAY READY FOR TRADE, MY JOINTS THE LIMBEREST JOINTS
    ON EARTH AND THE STERNEST JOINTS ON EARTH,

A KENTUCKIAN WALKING THE VALE OF THE ELKHORN IN MY DEER-SKIN LEGGINGS,
    A LOUISIANIAN OR GEORGIAN,

A BOATMAN OVER LAKES OR BAYS OR ALONG COASTS, A HOOSIER, BADGER, BUCKEYE;

AT HOME ON KANADIAN SNOW-SHOES OR UP IN THE BUSH,
    OR WITH FISHERMEN OFF NEWFOUNDLAND,

AT HOME IN THE FLEET OF ICE-BOATS, SAILING WITH THE REST AND TACKING,

AT HOME ON THE HILLS OF VERMONT OR IN THE WOODS OF MAINE, OR THE TEXAN RANCH,

Comrade of Californians, comrade of free North-Westerners,
  (loving their big proportions,)
Comrade of raftsmen and coalmen, comrade of all who shake hands
  and welcome to drink and meat,
A learner with the simplest, a teacher of the thoughtfullest,
A novice beginning yet experient of myriads of seasons,
Of every hue and caste am I, of every rank and religion,
A farmer, mechanic, artist, gentleman, sailor, quaker,
Prisoner, fancy-man, rowdy, lawyer, physician, priest.

I resist any thing better than my own diversity,
Breathe the air but leave plenty after me,
And am not stuck up, and am in my place.

(The moth and the fish-eggs are in their place,
The bright suns I see and the dark suns I cannot see are in their place,
The palpable is in its place and the impalpable is in its place.)

THE YELLOW ROSE OF TEXAS

ANONYMOUS, 1858

There's a yellow rose in Texas that I am going to see,
No other soldier knows her, no soldier only me;
She cried so when I left her, it like to broke my heart,
And if I ever find her we never more will part.

Chorus
She's the sweetest little flower this soldier ever knew,
Her eyes are bright as diamonds, they sparkle like the dew,
You may talk about your Dearest May, and sing of Rosa Lee,
But the yellow rose of Texas beats the belles of Tennessee.

Where the Rio Grande is flowing, and the starry skies are bright,
She walks along the river in the quiet summer night;
She thinks if I remember when we parted long ago,
I promised to come back again, and not to leave her so.

Chorus
Oh, now I'm going to find her, for my heart is full of woe,
And we'll sing the song together, that we sung so long ago;
We'll play the banjo gaily, and we'll sing the songs of yore,
And the yellow rose of Texas shall be mine forevermore.

The Civil War

When anti-slavery president Abraham Lincoln was elected, seven states seceded to form the Confederate States of America, with its own constitution and president, Jefferson Davis. On April 12, 1861 Davis' troops attacked the Union-held Fort Sumter in South Carolina, firing the shots that began the war.

Despite pressure, Lincoln insisted the war was more about preserving the Union than fighting slavery. After the battle at Antietam in September 1862, he reconsidered and issued the Emancipation Proclamation.

The first legal African-American regiment was the 54th Massachusetts. Many others followed: in all, 179,000 African Americans served in the Civil War.

William Tecumseh Sherman (1820–1891) led 100,000 Union troops through Georgia, leaving destruction in his wake.

Posing as a Confederate sympathizer, Virginian Elizabeth Van Lew passed information to the North. "Crazy Bet" also arranged prison escapes and hid fugitives.

At least 620,000 Americans died fighting the Civil War—that's more than in all wars America's fought since then, combined.

The Battle of Gettsyburg was the bloodiest of the war. Approximately 23,000 Union and 28,000 Confederate soldiers died before the North declared victory.

 Other major battles included Shiloh (24,000 killed) in April 1862, Second Manassas (25,000 killed) in August 1862, Chancellorsville (30,000 killed) in May 1863, and The Battle of the Wilderness (25,000 killed) in May 1864.

 The Civil War ended on April 9, 1865, with the Confederates' surrender at Appomattox, in Virginia.

The Civil War created more than 400,000 morphine-addicted veterans.

Robert E. Lee (1807–1870) commanded the Confederate forces. He led victories at Bull Run, Fredericksburg and Chancellorsville, before surrendering at Appomattox.

 Confederate President Jefferson Davis (1808–1889) was a congressman, war hero and secretary of war. He lost his citizenship after the war.

Ulysses S. Grant's (1822–1885) controversial leadership of the Union army caused heavy losses but won the war. He negotiated the South's surrender, and—as our 18th president— presided over the reconstruction.

 Confederate commander Thomas J. "Stonewall" Jackson (1824–1863) gained his nickname organizing troops into a line which withstood the Union assault at Bull Run. He died of injuries accidentally inflicted by his own men.

SULLIVAN BALLOU TO HIS WIFE SARAH

CAMP CLARK, WASHINGTON, JULY 14, 1861

Major Sullivan Ballou, of the 2nd Rhode Island Volunteers, wrote the following letter to his wife, Sarah, before the battle of Bull Run. The Union army was badly defeated in this first major battle of the war. 4,500 soldiers on both sides were killed, wounded or captured. Major Ballou was among the dead.

My very dear Sarah,

The indications are very strong that we shall move in a few days—perhaps tomorrow. Lest I should not be able to write again, I feel impelled to write a few lines that may fall under your eye when I shall be no more....

I have no misgivings about, or lack of confidence in, the cause in which I am engaged, and my courage does not halt or falter. I know how strongly American Civilization now leans on the triumph of the Government, and how great a debt we owe to those who went before us through the blood and sufferings of the Revolution. And I am willing—perfectly willing—to lay down all my joys in this life, to help maintain this Government, and to pay that debt....

Sarah my love for you is deathless. It seems to bind me with mighty cables that nothing but Omnipotence could break; and yet my love of Country comes over me like a strong wind and bears me unresistibly on with all these chains to the battlefield.

The memories of the blissful moments I have spent with you come creeping over me, and I feel most gratified to God and to you that I have enjoyed them so long. And hard it is for me to give them up and burn to ashes the hopes of future years, when, God willing, we might still have lived and loved together, and seen our sons grown up to honorable manhood around us. I have, I know, but few and small claims upon Divine Providence, but something whispers to me—perhaps it is the wafted prayer of my little Edgar—that I shall return to my loved ones unharmed. If I do not my dear Sarah, never forget how much I love you, and when my last breath escapes me on the battlefield, it will whisper your name. Forgive my many faults, and the many pains I have caused you. How thoughtless and foolish I have often times been! How gladly would I wash out with my tears every little spot upon your happiness, and struggle with all the misfortunes of this world to shield you and your children from

harm. But I cannot. I must watch you from the Spirit-land and hover near you, while you buffet the storm, with your precious little freight, and wait with sad patience till we meet to part no more.

But, O Sarah! if the dead can come back to this earth and flit unseen around those they loved, I shall always be near you; in the gladdest days and darkest nights, advised to your happiest scenes and gloomiest hours, *always, always,* and if there be a soft breeze upon your cheek, it shall be my breath; as the cool air fans your throbbing temple, it shall be my spirit passing by. Sarah do not mourn me dead; think I am gone and wait for thee, for we shall meet again.

As for my little boys—they will grow up as I have done, and never know a father's love and care. Little Willie is too young to remember me long, and my blue-eyed Edgar will keep my frolics with him among the dim memories of childhood. Sarah, I have unlimited confidence in your maternal care and your development of their character, and feel that God will bless you in your holy work.

Tell my two Mothers I call God's blessing upon them. O! Sarah. I wait for you there; come to me and lead thither my children.

Sullivan

BATTLE HYMN OF THE REPUBLIC

JULIA WARD HOWE, 1862

Mine eyes have seen the glory of the coming of the Lord:
He is trampling out the vintage where the grapes of wrath are stored;
He hath loosed the fateful lightning of his terrible swift sword:
   His truth is marching on.

   Chorus
   Glory, glory hallelujah,
   Glory, glory hallelujah,
   Glory, glory hallelujah,
   His truth is marching on.

I have seen Him in the watch-fires of a hundred circling camps;
They have builded Him an altar in the evening dews and damps;
I can read His righteous sentence by the dim and flaring lamps.
   His day is marching on.

I have read a fiery gospel, writ in burnished rows of steel:
"As ye deal with my contemners, so with you my grace shall deal;
Let the Hero, born of woman, crush the serpent with his heel,
   Since God is marching on."

He has sounded forth the trumpet that shall never call retreat;
He is sifting out the hearts of men before His judgment-seat:
Oh! be swift, my soul, to answer Him! be jubilant, my feet!
    Our God is marching on.

In the beauty of the lilies Christ was born across the sea,
With a glory in his bosom that transfigures you and me:
As he died to make men holy, let us die to make men free,
    While God is marching on.

The Emancipation Proclamation

ABRAHAM LINCOLN, JANUARY 1, 1863

Whereas, on the twenty-second day of September, in the year of our Lord one thousand eight hundred and sixty-two, a proclamation was issued by the President of the United States, containing, among other things, the following, to wit:

"That on the first day of January, in the year of our Lord one thousand eight hundred and sixty-three, all persons held as slaves within any State, or designated part of a State, the people whereof shall then be in rebellion against the United States, shall be then, thenceforward, and forever free; and the Executive Government of the United States, including the military and naval authority thereof, will recognize and maintain the freedom of such persons, and will do no act or acts to repress such persons, or any of them, in any efforts they may make for their actual freedom.

"That the Executive will, on the first day of January aforesaid, by proclamation, designate the States and parts of States, if any, in which the people thereof respectively shall then be in rebellion against the United States; and the fact that any State, or the people thereof, shall on that day be in good faith represented in the Congress of the United States by members chosen thereto at elections wherein a majority of the qualified voters of such State shall have participated, shall in the absence of strong countervailing testimony be deemed conclusive evidence that such State and the people thereof are not then in rebellion against the United States."

Now, therefore, I, Abraham Lincoln, President of the United States, by virtue of the power in me vested as commander-in-chief of the army and navy of the United States in time of actual armed rebellion against the authority and government of the United States, and as a fit and necessary war measure for suppressing said rebellion, do, on this first day of January, in the year of our Lord one thousand eight hundred and sixty-three, and in accordance with my purpose so to do, publicly proclaimed for the full period of 100 days from the day first above mentioned, order and designate as the States and parts of States wherein the people thereof, respectively, are this day in rebellion against the United States, the following, to wit:

Arkansas, Texas, Louisiana (except the parishes of St. Bernard, Plaquemines, Jefferson, St. John, St. Charles, St. James, Ascension, Assumption, Terre Bonne, Lafourche, St. Mary, St. Martin, and Orleans, including the city of New Orleans), Mississippi, Alabama, Florida, Georgia, South Carolina, North Carolina, and Virginia (except the forty-eight counties designated as West Virginia, and also the counties of Berkeley, Accomac, Northampton, Elizabeth City, York, Princess Ann, and Norfolk, including the cities of Norfolk and Portsmouth), and which excepted parts are for the present left precisely as if this proclamation were not issued.

And by virtue of the power and for the purpose aforesaid, I do order and declare that all persons held as slaves within said designated States and parts of States are, and henceforward shall be, free; and that the Executive Government of the United States, including the military and naval authorities thereof, will recognize and maintain the freedom of said persons.

And I hereby enjoin upon the people so declared to be free to abstain from all violence, unless in necessary self-defense; and I recommend to them that, in all cases when allowed, they labor faithfully for reasonable wages.

And I further declare and make known that such persons of suitable condition will be received into the armed service of the United States to garrison forts, positions, stations, and other places, and to man vessels of all sorts in said service.

And upon this act, sincerely believed to be an act of justice, warranted by the Constitution upon military necessity, I invoke the considerate judgment of mankind and the gracious favor of Almighty God.

African Americans

Born Isabella Baumfree, Sojourner Truth (1797–1883) was a New York slave freed when the state abolished slavery in 1828. She walked throughout the country speaking against slavery.

Frederick Douglass (1818–1895) was an escaped slave whose speeches were instrumental in the issuance of the Emancipation Proclamation.

Harriet Tubman (1820–1913) was a crucial figure in the Underground Railroad; an escaped slave herself, she risked her life to help bring more than 300 slaves into Canada.

Former slave Booker T. Washington (1856–1915) became a prominent educator and orator. In his position as advisor to two presidents, he was an early advocate of black self-reliance.

W. E. B. DuBois (1863–1963) was the first black to get a Ph.D. from Harvard. He later co-founded the National Association for the Advancement of Colored People (NAACP).

Edward Kennedy "Duke" Ellington (1899–1974) was a pianist, composer, bandleader and musical arranger who defined the sound of jazz with his complex and swinging melodies.

Thurgood Marshall (1908–1993) successfully argued the landmark *Brown v. Board of Education* for the NAACP. He went on to become the first African American Supreme Court Justice.

By refusing to give her bus seat to a white man in 1955, Rosa Parks (1913–) became the embodiment of resistance to the South's Jim Crow laws. Her gesture sparked a bus boycott that galvanized the civil rights movement.

In 1950 Gwendolyn Brooks (1917–2000) became the first black to win a Pulitzer Prize for her poetry collection, *Annie Allen*.

Known as the "First Lady of Song," Ella Fitzgerald's (1918–1996) interpretations defined the great jazz composers. She was also a visionary in the art of scat-singing—playing her voice like an instrument, with impeccable rhythm and pitch.

After a brief prison term, Malcolm Little became Malcolm X (1925–1965)—a leader of the Nation of Islam who preached black unity and empowerment. In 1964, he converted to orthodox Islam. He was assassinated by former Nation of Islam comrades a year later.

The Reverend Martin Luther King, Jr. (1929–1968) was an inspiring civil rights leader. He won the 1964 Nobel Peace Prize for advocating non-violence as the path to social change.

Talk show queen Oprah Winfrey (1954–) is one of the richest people in America. The award-winning media mogul and philanthropist also acts, edits her own magazine and produces films.

FROM

GONE WITH THE WIND

MARGARET MITCHELL, 1936

(SET AT THE END OF THE CIVIL WAR)

IN THE DAYS THAT FOLLOWED, Tara might have been Crusoe's desert island, so still it was, so isolated from the rest of the world. The world lay only a few miles away, but a thousand miles of tumbling waves might have stretched between Tara and Jonesboro and Fayetteville and Lovejoy, even between Tara and the neighbors' plantations. With the old horse dead, their one mode of conveyance was gone, and there was neither time nor strength for walking the weary red miles.

Sometimes, in the days of backbreaking work, in the desperate struggle for food and the never-ceasing care of the three sick girls, Scarlett found herself straining her ears for familiar sounds—the shrill laughter of the pickaninnies in the quarters, the creaking of wagons home from the fields, the thunder of Gerald's stallion tearing across the pasture, the crunching of carriage wheels on the drive and the gay voices of neighbors dropping in for an afternoon of gossip. But she listened in vain. The road lay still and deserted and never a cloud of red dust proclaimed the approach of visitors. Tara was an island in a sea of rolling green hills and red fields.

Gone with the Wind

Somewhere was the world and families who ate and slept safely under their own roofs. Somewhere girls in thrice-turned dresses were flirting gaily and singing "When This Cruel War Is Over," as she had done only a few weeks before. Somewhere there was a war and cannon booming and burning towns and men who rotted in hospitals amid sickening-sweet stinks. Somewhere a barefoot army in dirty homespun was marching, fighting, sleeping, hungry and weary with the weariness that comes when hope is gone. And somewhere the hills of Georgia were blue with Yankees, well-fed Yankees on sleek corn-stuffed horses.

Beyond Tara was the war and the world. But on the plantation the war and the world did not exist except as memories which must be fought back when they rushed to mind in moments of exhaustion. The world outside receded before the demands of empty and half-empty stomachs and life resolved itself into two related thoughts, food and how to get it.

THE GETTYSBURG ADDRESS

ABRAHAM LINCOLN
GETTYSBURG, PENNSYLVANIA, NOVEMBER 19, 1863

FOUR SCORE AND SEVEN YEARS AGO our fathers brought forth on this continent a new nation, conceived in liberty, and dedicated to the proposition that all men are created equal.

Now we are engaged in a great civil war, testing whether that nation or any nation so conceived and so dedicated can long endure. We are met on a great battle-field of that war. We have come to dedicate a portion of that field as a final resting place for those who here gave their lives that that nation might live. It is altogether fitting and proper that we should do this.

But in a larger sense, we cannot dedicate—we can not consecrate, we can not hallow—this ground. The brave men, living and dead, who struggled here, have consecrated it, far above our poor power to add or detract. The world will little note nor long remember what we say here, but it can never forget what they did here. It is for us the living, rather, to be dedicated here to the unfinished work which they who fought here have thus far so nobly advanced. It is rather for us to be here dedicated to the great task remaining before us—that from these honored dead we take increased devotion to that cause for which they gave the last full measure of devotion—that we here highly resolve that these dead shall not have died in vain—that this nation under God, shall have a new birth of freedom—and that government of the people, by the people, for the people shall not perish from the earth.

GENERAL ROBERT E. LEE TO HIS ARMY

HEADQUARTERS, ARMY OF NORTHERN VIRGINIA
APRIL 10, 1865

On April 9, 1865, Confederate General Robert E. Lee surrendered to Union General Ulysses S. Grant. The following day, he addressed his army.

After four years of arduous service, marked by unsurpassed courage and fortitude, the Army of Northern Virginia has been compelled to yield to overwhelming numbers and resources. I need not tell the survivors of so many hard-fought battles, who have remained steadfast to the last, that I have consented to this result from no distrust of them; but, feeling that valor and devotion could accomplish nothing that could compensate for the loss that would have attended the continuation of the contest, I have determined to avoid the useless sacrifice of those whose past services have endeared them to their countrymen. By the terms of the agreement, officers and men can return to their homes and remain there until exchanged. You will take with you the satisfaction that proceeds from the consciousness of duty faithfully performed; and I earnestly pray that a merciful God will extend to you His blessing and protection. With an increasing admiration of your constancy and devotion to your country, and a grateful remembrance of your kind and generous consideration of myself, I bid you an affectionate farewell.

R. E. Lee, General

THE MARINES' HYMN

TRADITIONAL, CIRCA 1870S

From the Halls of Montezuma
To the shores of Tripoli
We fight our country's battles
In the air, on land and sea.

First to fight for right and freedom
And to keep our honor clean;
We are proud to claim the title of
United States Marine.

Our flag's unfurled to every breeze
from dawn to setting sun.
We have fought in every clime and place,
where we could take a gun.

In the snow of far off northern lands
and in sunny tropic scenes,
You will find us always on the job,
The United States Marines.

Here's health to you and to our Corps
which we are proud to serve.
In many a strife we've fought for life
and never lost our nerve.

If the Army and the Navy ever look on
heaven's scenes,
they will find the streets are guarded by
United States Marines.

BELOVED

TONI MORRISON, 1987 (SET IN THE 1870s)

Before 124 and everybody in it had closed down, veiled over and shut away; before it had become the plaything of spirits and the home of the chafed, 124 had been a cheerful, buzzing house where Baby Suggs, holy, loved, cautioned, fed, chastised and soothed. Where not one but two pots simmered on the stove; where the lamp burned all night long. Strangers rested there while children tried on their shoes. Messages were left there, for whoever needed them was sure to stop in one day soon. Talk was low and to the point—for Baby Suggs, holy, didn't approve of extra. "Everything depends on knowing how much," she said, and "Good is knowing when to stop."

It was in front of *that* 124 that Sethe climbed off a wagon, her newborn tied to her chest, and felt for the first time the wide arms of her mother-in-law, who had made it to Cincinnati. Who decided that, because slave life had "busted her legs, back, head, eyes, hands, kidneys, womb and tongue," she had nothing left to make a living with but her heart—which she put to work at once. Accepting no title of honor before her name, but allowing a small caress after it, she became an unchurched preacher, one who visited pulpits and opened her great heart to those who could use it. In winter and fall she carried it to AME's and Baptists, Holinesses and Sanctifieds, the Church of the Redeemer and the Redeemed. Uncalled, unrobed, unanointed, she let her great heart beat in their presence. When warm weather came, Baby Suggs, holy, followed by every black man, woman and child who could make it through, took her great heart to the Clearing—a wide-open place cut deep in the woods nobody knew for what at the end of a path known only to deer and whoever cleared the land in the first place. In the heat of every Saturday afternoon, she sat in the clearing while the people waited among the trees.

After situating herself on a huge flat-sided rock, Baby Suggs bowed her head and prayed silently. The company watched her from the trees. They knew she was ready when she put her stick down. Then she shouted, "Let the children come!" and they ran from the trees toward her.

"Let your mothers hear you laugh," she told them, and the woods rang. The adults looked on and could not help smiling.

Then "Let the grown men come," she shouted. They stepped out one by one from among the ringing trees.

"Let your wives and your children see you dance," she told them, and groundlife shuddered under their feet.

Finally she called the women to her. "Cry," she told them. "For the living and the dead. Just cry." And without covering their eyes the women let loose.

It started that way: laughing children, dancing men, crying women and then it got mixed up. Women stopped crying and danced; men sat down and cried; children danced, women laughed, children cried until, exhausted and riven, all and each lay about the Clearing damp and gasping for breath. In the silence that followed, Baby Suggs, holy, offered up to them her great big heart.

She did not tell them to clean up their lives or to go and sin no more. She did not tell them they were the blessed of the earth, its inheriting meek or its glorybound pure.

She told them that the only grace they could have was the grace they could imagine. That if they could not see it, they would not have it.

BELOVED

"Here," she said, "in this here place, we flesh; flesh that weeps, laughs; flesh that dances on bare feet in grass. Love it. Love it hard. Yonder they do not love your flesh. They despise it. They don't love your eyes; they'd just as soon pick em out. No more do they love the skin on your back. Yonder they flay it. And O my people they do not love your hands. Those they only use, tie, bind, chop off and leave empty. Love your hands! Love them. Raise them up and kiss them. Touch others with them, pat them together, stroke them on your face 'cause they don't love that either. *You* got to love it, *you!* And no, they ain't in love with your mouth. Yonder, out there, they will see it broken and break it again. What you say out of it they will not heed. What you scream from it they do not hear. What you put into it to nourish your body they will snatch away and give you leavins instead. No, they don't love your mouth. *You* got to love it. This is flesh I'm talking about here. Flesh that needs to be loved. Feet that need to rest and to dance; backs that need support; shoulders that need arms, strong arms I'm telling you. And O my people, out yonder, hear me, they do not love your neck unnoosed and straight. So love your neck; put a hand on it, grace it, stroke it and hold it up. And all your inside parts that they'd just as soon slop for hogs, you got to love them. The dark, dark liver—love it, love it, and the beat and beating heart, love that too. More than eyes or feet. More than lungs that have yet to draw free air. More than your life-hold-

ing womb and your life-giving private parts, hear me now, love your heart. For this is the prize." Saying no more, she stood up then and danced with her twisted hip the rest of what her heart had to say while the others opened their mouths and gave her the music. Long notes held until the four-part harmony was perfect enough for their deeply loved flesh.

BISCUITS & GRAVY

Today's basic biscuit is much easier on the jaw than the original "hardtack" biscuits served as Civil War rations. Called "tooth dullers" by the soldiers, they were served with a rich dipping gravy whenever possible.

Biscuits

$^1/_2$ cup lukewarm water

1 teaspoon active dry yeast

2 tablespoons sugar

2 $^1/_2$ cups unbleached all-purpose flour

1 teaspoon baking powder

1 teaspoon salt

$^1/_4$ cup vegetable shortening

4 tablespoons butter, chilled

$^3/_4$ cup milk or buttermilk

1. In a small mixing bowl, whisk together the warm water, yeast and sugar. Set the mixture aside for 30 minutes. In a medium bowl, whisk together the flour, baking powder and salt. Cut in the shortening and butter, and mix until rough and crumbly.

2. Pour the milk or buttermilk into the yeast mixture, and add this to the dry ingredients. Fold together gently until the mixture leaves the sides of the bowl and becomes cohesive.

3. Turn the dough out onto a lightly floured work surface. Knead gently six times and form a ball. Pat it out until the dough is about $^1/_2$″ thick. Use a glass to cut the dough into as many biscuits as you can. Gather the scraps gently and do it again.

4. Put the biscuits on a lightly greased or parchment-lined cookie sheet. Cover with a damp towel and let rise in a warm place for approximately 1 hour.

5. Preheat oven to 400° F.

6. Bake biscuits for 10–12 minutes.

Serves 6 to 8.

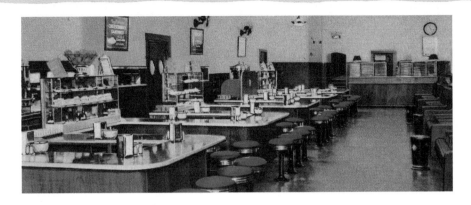

Gravy

1 pound pork
breakfast sausage,
bulk style,
chopped up

2 tablespoons flour

1 cup milk

salt and pepper
to taste

1. Fry the sausage until it is brown,
   breaking it up as you cook it.

2. Separate the cooked sausage from the drippings.
   Set the sausage aside.

3. Heat the drippings over a medium flame and
   slowly whisk in as much flour as there are drippings. Whisk and let bubble for 2–3 minutes.
   If the gravy is dry at this point, add some butter.

4. Add the milk, stirring vigorously, and bring it to a
   low boil. Simmer until it thickens (about 5 minutes).
   If it is too thick, add more milk. Add the sausage
   bits, and salt and pepper to taste.

   Pour over the warm biscuits or
   serve the gravy on the side.

Women

Pocahontas (1595–1617), daughter of a powerful Powhatan chief, helped improve Indian-settler relations by saving the life of settler John Smith. She later married Englishman John Rolfe and traveled to Britain, where she died of smallpox.

Dolley Madison (1768–1849) was a young widow when she married 43-year-old James Madison. She saved the original drafts of the Constitution and the Declaration of Independence from a White House fire.

Elizabeth Cady Stanton (1815–1902) was a writer and orator; Susan B. Anthony (1820–1906) a tactician and organizer. Together they influenced the legislation granting women property rights and, ultimately, the vote.

Elizabeth Blackwell (1821–1910) was the first American woman to earn a medical degree.

Red Cross founder Clara Barton's (1821–1912) fame grew from her campaign to provide care and medical supplies to wounded Civil War soldiers.

Planned Parenthood founder Margaret Sanger (1879–1966) educated women about birth control, campaigned to make methods available, and suffered censorship, jail and lawsuits.

Elected to the House in 1916, Montanan Jeannette Rankin (1880–1973) was America's first congresswoman.

✶

Devoted to helping others, First Lady Eleanor Roosevelt (1884–1962) campaigned for human, women's, and civil rights, and for the young, the poor and democracy.

✶

Amelia Earhart (1897–1937), the first woman passenger to fly the Atlantic, later flew it solo—in a record 14 hours, 56 minutes. In 1937, she vanished during an attempt to fly around the world.

✶

Colonel Oveta Culp Hobby (1905–1995) was the first female army colonel. Appointed to create a place in the army for women, she led the newly-created Women's Army Corps.

✶

Betty Friedan (1921–) wrote *The Feminine Mystique*, founded the National Organization for Women (NOW) and fought for the Equal Rights Amendment.

✶

Marilyn Monroe (1926–1962) was one of the 20th century's most famous faces. Christened Norma Jeane Baker, she starred in such films as *Some Like it Hot* and *The Misfits*.

✶

Singer Leontyne Price (1927–) debuted at the Metropolitan Opera House in 1961. Her honors include 18 Grammys and the Presidential Medal of Freedom.

✶

First Lady Jacqueline Bouvier Kennedy Onassis (1929–1994), infused the White House with style. After her husband's assassination, she moved to New York with her children and became a book editor.

✶

As a writer, journalist and activist for women's rights, Gloria Steinem (1934–) founded *Ms. Magazine*.

"ARE WOMEN PERSONS?"

SUSAN B. ANTHONY, JUNE 1873

In the 1872 presidential election, Susan B. Anthony was arrested and fined for voting illegally, along with a group of women. The incident served well to publicize her cause, which she defended in public speeches.

FRIENDS AND FELLOW CITIZENS, I stand before you tonight under indictment for the alleged crime of having voted at the last presidential election, without having a lawful right to vote. It shall be my work this evening to prove to you that in thus voting, I not only committed no crime but, instead, simply exercised my citizen's rights, guaranteed to me and all United States citizens by the National Constitution, beyond the power of any State to deny....

The preamble of the federal Constitution says:

"We, the people of the United States, in order to form a more perfect union, establish justice, insure domestic tranquillity, provide for the common defense, promote the general welfare, and secure the blessings of liberty to ourselves and our posterity, do ordain and establish this Constitution for the United States of America."

It was we, the people; not we, the white male citizens; nor yet we, the male citizens; but we, the whole people, who formed the Union. And

we formed it, not to give the blessings of liberty, but to secure them; not to the half of ourselves and the half of our posterity, but to the whole people—women as well as men. And it is a downright mockery to talk to women of their enjoyment of the blessings of liberty while they are denied the use of the only means of securing them provided by this democratic-republican government—the ballot....

For any state to make sex a qualification that must ever result in the disfranchisement of one entire half of the people is to pass a bill of attainder, or an ex post facto law, and is therefore a violation of the supreme law of the land. By it the blessings of liberty are forever withheld from women and their female posterity. To them this government has no just powers derived from the consent of the governed. To them this government is not a democracy. It is not a republic. It is an odious aristocracy; a hateful oligarchy of sex; the most hateful aristocracy ever established on the face of the globe;...which makes father, brothers, husband, sons, the oligarchs over the mothers and sisters, the wife and daughters, of every household—which ordains all men sovereigns, all women subjects, carries dissension, discord, and rebellion into every home of the nation....

The only question left to be settled now is: Are women persons? And I hardly believe any of our opponents will have the hardihood to say they are not. Being persons, then, women are citizens; and no state has a right to make any law, or to enforce any old law, that shall abridge their privileges or immunities. Hence, every discrimination against women in the constitutions and laws of the several states is today null and void, precisely as is every one against Negroes....

We no longer petition Legislature or Congress to give us the right to vote. We appeal to women everywhere to exercise their too long neglected "citizen's right to vote." We appeal to the inspectors of election everywhere to receive the votes of all United States citizens as it is their duty to do....

And it is on this line that we propose to fight our battle for the ballot— all peaceably, but nevertheless persistently through to complete triumph, when all United States citizens shall be recognized as equals before the law.

HOME ON THE RANGE

BREWSTER HIGHLEY, CIRCA 1876

O give me a home where the buffalo roam,
Where the deer and the antelope play.
Where seldom is heard a discouraging word,
And the skies are not cloudy all day.

Chorus
  Home, home on the range,
  Where the deer and the antelope play.
  Where seldom is heard a discouraging word,
  And the skies are not cloudy all day.

Where the air is so pure, the zephyrs so free,
And the breezes so balmy and light.
Then I would not exchange my home on the range
For all of your cities so bright.

The redman was pressed from this part of the West,
And he's likely no more to return
To the banks of the Red River, where seldom, if ever,
Their flickering campfires burn.

How often at night when the heavens are bright
With the light from the glittering stars,
Have I stood there amazed, and asked as I gazed,
If their glory exceeds that of ours.

I love the wild flowers in this dear land of ours,
And the curlew I love to hear scream.
I love the white rocks and the antelope flocks
That graze on the mountaintops green.

O give me a land where the bright diamond sand
Flows leisurely down the stream.
Where the graceful white swan goes gliding along,
Like a maid in a heavenly dream.

That I would not exchange my home on the range,
Where the deer and the antelope play.
Where seldom is heard a discouraging word,
And the skies are not cloudy all day.

The Southwest

✳

Though Flagstaff, Arizona's Lowell Observatory was founded primarily to explore the possibility of life on Mars, it's better known for the discovery of the planet Pluto, in 1930.

✳

Georgia O'Keefe's (1887–1986) paintings of stark skulls and vibrant desert vistas near her beloved New Mexico home immortalized the light and landscapes of the Southwest.

✳

Each year Las Vegas is visited by 30 million people, who lose about $8 billion gambling, and spend another $8 billion on the state's tourism industry.

✳

Las Vegas's chapels perform 110,000 marriages annually— about 300 a day.

✳

Construction of the Hoover Dam, on the Colorado River, required more than 5 million barrels of cement.

✳

The first atomic bomb was detonated in Alamogordo, New Mexico, on July 16, 1945.

✳

Santa Fe, New Mexico was established by the Spaniards in 1610.

✳

On April 18, 1934, America's first laundromat opened in Fort Worth, Texas.

✳

Bracken Cave in Texas is home to the largest bat maternity colony in the world. Its 20 million Mexican free-tailed bats can consume up to 500,000 pounds of insects on a single summer night.

Covering 1300 square miles, Texas' King Ranch, founded in 1853, is bigger than the state of Rhode Island.

In 1977 the Texas State Legislature proclaimed chili the state's official dish.

"Juneteenth" is a real holiday. On June 19th, 1865, Texas slaves were freed under General Order #3. Today that's still celebrated in Texas, Louisiana, Arkansas and Oklahoma.

Considered the deadliest natural disaster in U.S. history, the 1900 hurricane that hit Galveston, Texas killed more than 6,000 people. The toll was greater than those of the Great Chicago Fire, the Johnstown, PA Flood and the San Francisco Earthquake and Fire—combined.

Dr. Pepper, America's first soft drink, was created in 1885 in Waco, Texas by Charles Alderton, who named it after his first boss.

Texas is the only state to allow absentee voting from anywhere in the universe. The first person to take advantage of that was astronaut David Wolf— whose ballot came from the space station Mir, in 1997.

THE AMERICAN

O N A BRILLIANT DAY IN MAY, in the year 1868, a gentleman was reclining at his ease on the great circular divan which at that period occupied the centre of the Salon Carré, in the Museum of the Louvre....

An observer, with anything of an eye for national types, would have had no difficulty in determining the local origin of this undeveloped connoisseur, and indeed such an observer might have felt a certain humorous relish of the almost ideal completeness with which he filled out the national mould. The gentleman on the divan was a powerful specimen of an American. But he was not only a fine American; he was in the first place, physically, a fine man. He appeared to possess that kind of health and strength which, when found in perfection, are the most impressive—the physical capital which the owner does nothing to "keep up." If he was a muscular Christian, it was quite without knowing it. If it was necessary to walk to a remote spot, he walked, but he had never known himself to "exercise." He had no theory with regard to cold bathing or the

THE AMERICAN

use of Indian clubs; he was neither an oarsman, a rifleman, nor a fencer—
he had never had time for these amusements—and he was quite unaware
that the saddle is recommended for certain forms of indigestion. He was
by inclination a temperate man; but he had supped the night before
his visit to the Louvre at the Café Anglais—someone had told him it
was an experience not to be omitted—and he had slept none the less
the sleep of the just. His usual attitude and carriage were of a rather
relaxed and lounging kind, but when, under a special inspiration, he
straightened himself, he looked like a grenadier on parade. He never
smoked. He had been assured—such things are said—that cigars were
excellent for the health, and he was quite capable of believing it; but
he knew as little about tobacco as about homoeopathy. He had a very
well-formed head, with a shapely, symmetrical balance of the frontal
and the occipital development, and a good deal of straight, rather dry
brown hair. His complexion was brown, and his nose had a bold, well-
marked arch. His eye was of a clear, cold gray, and, save for a rather
abundant moustache, he was clean-shaved. He had the flat jaw and
sinewy neck which are frequent in the American type; but the traces
of national origin are a matter of expression even more than of feature,
and it was in this respect that our friend's countenance was supremely

THE AMERICAN

eloquent. The discriminating observer we have been supposing might, however, perfectly have measured its expressiveness, and yet have been at a loss to describe it. It had that typical vagueness which is not vacuity, that blankness which is not simplicity, that look of being committed to nothing in particular, of standing in an attitude of general hospitality to the chances of life, of being very much at one's own disposal, so characteristic of many American faces. It was our friend's eye that chiefly told his story; an eye in which innocence and experience were singularly blended. It was full of contradictory suggestions; and though it was by no means the glowing orb of a hero of romance, you could find in it almost anything you looked for. Frigid and yet friendly, frank yet cautious, shrewd yet credulous, positive yet sceptical, confident yet shy, extremely intelligent and extremely good-humoured, there was something vaguely defiant in its concessions, and something profoundly reassuring in its reserve. The cut of this gentleman's moustache, with the two premature wrinkles in the cheek above it, and the fashion of his garments, in which an exposed shirt-front and a cerulean cravat played perhaps an obtrusive part, completed the conditions of his identity.

"I WILL FIGHT NO MORE FOREVER"

CHIEF JOSEPH, NEZ PERCÉ
SNAKE CREEK, MONTANA, OCTOBER 5, 1877

Chief Joseph, leader of the Nez Percé, steadfastly refused the white man's attempts to move his people off their Oregon land and onto a reservation. When the tribe was finally forced to leave, they attempted to escape to Canada. But after travelling more than a thousand miles in bad conditions, they were trapped some thirty miles from the border. Chief Joseph made this speech upon their surrender.

TELL GENERAL HOWARD I know his heart. What he told me before, I have it in my heart. I am tired of fighting. Our chiefs are killed; Looking Glass is dead, Ta-Hool-Hool-Shute is dead. The old men are all dead. It is the young men who say "Yes" or "No." He who led on the young men is dead. It is cold, and we have no blankets; the little children are freezing to death. My people, some of them, have run away to the hills, and have no blankets, no food. No one knows where they are—perhaps freezing to death. I want to have time to look for my children, and see how many of them I can find. Maybe I shall find them among the dead. Hear me, my chiefs! I am tired; my heart is sick and sad. From where the sun now stands I will fight no more forever.

THE WHOLE WORLD IS COMING

LAKOTA GHOST DANCE SONG, CIRCA 1880

The whole world is coming.
A nation is coming, a nation is coming,
The Eagle has brought the message to the tribe.
The father says so, the father says so.
Over the whole earth they are coming.
The buffalo are coming, the buffalo are coming,
The crow has brought the message to the tribe,
The father says so, the father says so.

The Wild West

On October 26, 1881, the Earp brothers (Wyatt, Virgil, and Morgan) and Doc Holliday faced down the Clanton Gang in a 30-second hail of bullets behind the OK Corral in Tombstone, Arizona. When it was over, Virgil and Morgan were wounded and three outlaws lay dead.

Doc Holliday (1851–1887) was a dentist by trade who moved West for his health.

Wyatt Earp (1848–1929) was a gambler and a law man who roamed the West from Illinois to Alaska.

Born Martha Jane Cannary in Princeton, Missouri, Calamity Jane (1852–1903) was orphaned as a young girl. She made her way working anywhere from mining camps to dance halls. A drinker, talker and smoker who shot like a man, she claimed to have married Wild Bill Hickok.

There was truth to the legends surrounding Wild Bill Hickok (1837–1876): a farmhand, stagecoach driver and hired gun, he worked as a Union army spy and served as a Marshall on the rough frontier after the Civil War.

Crazy Horse (1844–1877), chief of the Oglala Sioux, refused to be pushed onto a reservation. He united Sioux and Cheyenne forces to defeat General Custer and his troops at Little Bighorn, but ultimately surrendered in order to survive.

Geronimo (1829–1909), though not a chief, was recognized as a leader of the Chiricahua Apache. After being forced onto a barren reservation in Arizona, he led a number of revolts. Years of conflict ended in Geronimo's surrender, and he died in detention.

General George Armstrong Custer (1839–1876) earned his reputation in the campaigns against the Indians in South Dakota and Montana, as well as in the Civil War. He was killed at Little Bighorn, where his men were defeated by Lakota, Cheyenne and Arapaho warriors.

Teton Sioux Chief Sitting Bull (1831–1890) was instrumental in annihilating General Custer's attacking forces, but lived on to see his people surrender and move to reservations. Late in his life, he traveled with Buffalo Bill's Wild West show.

"Buffalo" Bill Cody (1846–1917) was a champion buffalo hunter, army scout and founder of Buffalo Bill's Wild West, a traveling show that began the rodeo and toured America and Europe.

CALAMITY JANE TO
HER DAUGHTER, JANEY
SEPTEMBER, 1880

Calamity Jane's daughter was raised by family friends. Though Jane often visited, her daughter never knew her true identity. This letter was part of a journal of letters Jane wrote to her daughter, but never sent.

Janey, a letter from your Daddy Jim came today and another picture of you. Your birthday is this month, you are 7 years old. I like this picture of you...Your expression [is] exactly like your father's....

Your picture brought back all the years I have lived with your Father and recalled how jealous I was of him. I feel like writing about him tonight so I will tell you some things you should know. I met James Butlet Hickock, 'Wild Bill,' in 1870 near Abeline, Kansas. I heard a bunch of outlaws planning to kill him. I couldn't get to where my horse was so I crawled on my hands and knees through the brush past the outlaws for over a mile and reached the old shack where he was staying that night. I told him and he hid me back of the door while he shot it out with them. They hit him, cutting open the top of his head and then they heard him fall and lit matches to see if he was dead. Bill killed them all. I'll never forget what he looked like with

blood running down his face while he used two guns. He never aimed and I guess he was never known to have missed anyone he aimed at, I mean wanted to kill, and he only shot in self-defence. Then he was quite sure. I nursed him several days and then while on the trip to Abeline we met Rev. Sipes and Rev. Warren and we were married. There will be lots of fools doubt that but I will leave you plenty of proof that we were. You were not a woods colt Janey. Don't let any of those pusgullied [erased] ever get busy with that lie....

Don't let jealousy get you Janey. It kills love and all the nice things in life. It drove your father from me. When I lost him I lost everything I ever loved except you. I gave him a divorce so he could marry Agnes Lake. I was trying to make amends for the jealous times and my spells of meanness. If she had loved him she would have come out here with him but she didn't and I was glad to have him again even if he was married and she was so far away. I always excused our sin by knowing he was mine long before he was hers. A man can love two women at one time. He loved her and still he loved me. He loved me because of you Janey.

CHILI & CORN BREAD

It was once said of legendary bad boy Billy the Kid that "anybody who eats chili can't be that bad." Popularized on the Texas cattle drives, chili's accompaniment, corn bread, was invented when earlier settlers had to substitute Indian corn meal for wheat in their breads.

Chili

1 cup dry red kidney beans or 3 cups canned cooked beans

1 lb. ground round

2 yellow onions, diced

1 small bottle ketchup

2 cans tomatoes (14.5 ounces each) or 4 cups diced and stewed tomatoes

$^1/_8$ teaspoon cayenne pepper (or more if you like it spicy)

$^1/_8$ teaspoon chili powder (or more if you like it spicy)

salt and pepper to taste

Corn Bread

1 $^1/_2$ cups yellow cornmeal

$^1/_2$ cup all-purpose flour

1 cup buttermilk

1 can (8 ounces) creamed corn

$^1/_2$ cup shredded cheddar cheese

$^1/_2$ teaspoon chili powder

2 tablespoons vegetable oil

2 teaspoons baking powder

1 teaspoon sugar

1 teaspoon salt

$^1/_2$ teaspoon baking soda

2 large eggs, mixed

1. If you are using dry beans, soak them overnight in 3 cups of cold water.

2. Simmer the beans for 1 1/2–2 hours on the stovetop until tender.

3. Cook the meat and the onions over a medium-high flame, stirring until the meat is brown, crumbled and cooked through.

4. Add the meat and onions to the beans, along with the ketchup, tomatoes and spices. Transfer to a casserole dish.

5. Heat the oven to 450° F.

6. Mix all the corn bread ingredients together in a large bowl. Stir well until completely blended and pour the batter on top of the chili.

7. Bake for 20 minutes until golden brown and serve with a salad.

Serves 6.

ADVENTURES OF HUCKLEBERRY FINN

MARK TWAIN, 1885

We had mountains on the Missouri shore and heavy timber on the Illinois side, and the channel was down the Missouri shore at that place, so we warn't afraid of anybody running across us. We laid there all day and watched the rafts and steamboats spin down the Missouri shore, and up-bound steamboats fight the big river in the middle....

When it was beginning to come on dark, we poked our heads out of the cottonwood thicket and looked up, and down, and across; nothing in sight; so Jim took up some of the top planks of the raft and built a snug wigwam to get under in blazing weather and rainy, and to keep the things dry. Jim made a floor for the wigwam, and raised it a foot or more above the level of the raft, so now the blankets and all the traps was out of the reach of steamboat waves. Right in the middle of the wigwam we made a layer of dirt about five or six inches deep with a frame around it for to hold it to its place; this was to build a fire on in sloppy weather or chilly; the wigwam would keep it from being seen. We made an extra steering oar, too, because one of the others might get broke, on a snag or something. We fixed up a short forked stick to hang the old lantern on; because we must always light the lantern whenever we see a steamboat coming down stream, to keep from getting run over; but we wouldn't have to light it for up-stream boats unless we see we was in what they call a "crossing"; for the river was pretty high yet, very low banks being still a little under water; so up-bound boats didn't always run the channel, but hunted easy water.

This second night we run between seven and eight hours, with a current that was making over four mile an hour. We catched fish, and talked, and we took a swim now and then to keep off sleepiness. It was kind of solemn, drifting down the big still river, laying on our backs looking up at the stars, and we didn't ever feel like talking loud, and it warn't often that we laughed, only a little kind of a low chuckle. We had might good weather, as a general thing, and nothing ever happened to us at all, that night, nor the next, nor the next.

Every night we passed towns, some of them away up on black hillsides, nothing but just a shiny bed of lights, not a house could you see. The fifth night we passed St. Louis, and it was like the whole world lit up. In St. Petersburg they used to say there was twenty or thirty thousand people in St. Louis, but I never believed it till I see that wonderful spread of lights at two o'clock that still night. There warn't a sound there; everybody was asleep.

Every night, now, I used to slip ashore, towards ten o'clock, at some little village, and buy ten or fifteen cents' worth of meal or bacon or other stuff to eat; and sometimes I lifted a chicken that warn't roosting comfortable, and took him along. Pap always said, take a chicken when you get a chance, because if you don't want him yourself you can easy find somebody that does, and a good deed ain't ever forgot. I never see pap when he didn't want the chicken himself, but that is what he used to say, anyway.

Mornings, before daylight, I slipped into corn fields and borrowed a watermelon, or a mushmelon, or a punkin, or some new corn, or things of that kind. Pap always said it warn't no harm to borrow things, if you was meaning to pay them back, sometime; but the widow said it warn't anything but a soft name for stealing, and no decent body would do it. Jim said he reckoned the widow was partly right and pap was partly right; so the best way would be for us to pick out two or three things from the list and say we wouldn't borrow them anymore—then he reckoned it wouldn't be no harm to borrow the others. So we talked it over all one night, drifting along down the river, trying to make up our minds whether to drop the watermelons, or the cantelopes, or the mushmelons, or what. But towards daylight we got it all settled satisfactory, and concluded to drop crab-apples and p'simmons. We warn't feeling just right, before that, but it was all comfortable now. I was glad the way it come out, too, because crabapples ain't ever good, and the p'simmons wouldn't be ripe for two or three months yet.

We shot a water-fowl, now and then, that got up too early in the morning or didn't go to bed early enough in the evening. Take it all around, we lived pretty high.

The Midwest

Our quintet of Great Lakes—
Lake Superior, Lake Michigan,
Lake Huron, Lake Erie
and Lake Ontario—holds 18%
of the world's fresh water.

More than 6,000 wrecked
ships can be found at the
bottom of the Great Lakes.

Michigan borders four
of the five Great Lakes.
It gets its name from
the Native American word
michigana, which
means "great or large lake."

Idaho produces 138 million
pounds of potatoes a year.

The citizens of Hell, Michigan
take great pride in the fact that
in the winter of 1995–96,
Hell actually did freeze over.

Nebraska is the only state to have
a unicameral, or one-house,
legislature. Members are elected
to it without party designation,
and have been since 1937.

The Great Fire of Chicago in 1871 did start at around 9 PM on October 8, in the O'Leary's cow barn. But the enduring legend that Mrs. O'Leary's cow was responsible for leveling the entire city (by kicking over a lantern) has never been proven.

In 1887, Argonia, Kansas elected the first female mayor in the nation: Susanna Salter.

Covering only 36,185 square miles, Indiana is the smallest state west of the Appalachian Mountains (not counting Hawaii).

Many Wisconsin towns bill themselves as the capital of something, including:

GREEN BAY—"The Toilet Paper Capital of the World."

BELLEVILLE—"The UFO Capital of Wisconsin."

BLOOMER—"The Jump Rope Capital of the World."

BOSCOBEL—"The Turkey Capital of Wisconsin."

MONROE—"The Swiss Cheese Capital of the World."

MOUNT HOREB—"The Troll Capital of the World."

SHEBOYGAN—"The Bratwurst Capital of the World."

SOMERSET—"The Inner Tubing Capital of the World."

The New Colossus

Emma Lazarus, 1883
inscribed on The Statue of Liberty in 1901

Not like the brazen giant of Greek fame,
With conquering limbs astride from land to land;
Here at our sea-washed, sunset gates shall stand
A mighty woman with a torch, whose flame
Is imprisoned lightning, and her name
Mother of Exiles. From her beacon-hand
Glows world-wide welcome; her mild eyes command
The air-bridged harbor that twin cities frame.
"Keep, ancient lands, your storied pomp!" cries she
With silent lips. "Give me your tired, your poor,
Your huddled masses yearning to breathe free,
The wretched refuse of your teeming shore.
Send these, the homeless, tempest-tost to me,
I lift my lamp beside the golden door!"

CASEY AT THE BAT

ERNEST LAWRENCE THAYER, 1888

The outlook wasn't brilliant for the Mudville nine that day:
The score stood four to two with but one inning more to play.
And then when Cooney died at first, and Barrows did the same,
A sickly silence fell upon the patrons of the game.

A straggling few got up to go in deep despair. The rest
Clung to that hope which springs eternal in the human breast;
They thought if only Casey could but get a whack at that—
We'd put up even money now with Casey at the bat.

But Flynn preceded Casey, as did also Jimmy Blake,
And the former was a lulu and the latter was a cake;
So upon that stricken multitude grim melancholy sat,
For there seemed but little chance of Casey's getting to the bat.

But Flynn let drive a single, to the wonderment of all,
And Blake, the much despis-ed, tore the cover off the ball;

And when the dust had lifted, and the men saw what had occurred,
There was Jimmy safe at second and Flynn a-hugging third.

Then from 5,000 throats and more there rose a lusty yell;
It rumbled through the valley, it rattled in the dell;
It knocked upon the mountain and recoiled upon the flat,
For Casey, might Casey, was advancing to the bat.

There was ease in Casey's manner as he stepped into his place;
There was pride in Casey's bearing and a smile on Casey's face.
And when, responding to the cheers, he lightly doffed his hat,
No stranger in the crowd could doubt 'twas Casey at the bat.

Ten thousand eyes were on him as he rubbed his hands with dirt;
Five thousand tongues applauded when he wiped them on his shirt.
Then while the writhing pitcher ground the ball into his hip,
Defiance gleamed in Casey's eye, a sneer curled Casey's lip.

And now the leather-covered sphere came hurtling through the air,
And Casey stood a-watching it in haughty grandeur there.
Close by the sturdy batsman the ball unheeded sped—
"That ain't my style," said Casey. "Strike one," the umpire said.

From the benches black with people, there went up a muffled roar,
Like the beating of the storm-waves on a stern and distant shore.
"Kill him! Kill the umpire!" shouted some one on the stand;
And it's likely they'd have killed him had not Casey raised his hand.

With a smile of Christian charity great Casey's visage shone;
He stilled the rising tumult; he bade the game go on;
He signaled to the pitcher, and once more the spheroid flew;
But Casey still ignored it, and the umpire said, "Strike two."

GRANT WRIGHT

"Fraud!" cried the maddened thousands, and echo answered fraud;
But one scornful look from Casey and the audience was awed.
They saw his face grow stern and cold, they saw his muscles strain,
And they knew that Casey wouldn't let that ball go by again.

The sneer is gone from Casey's lip, his teeth are clenched in hate;
He pounds with cruel violence his bat upon the plate.
And now the pitcher holds the ball, and now he lets it go,
And now the air is shattered by the force of Casey's blow.

Oh, somewhere in this favored land the sun is shining bright;
The band is playing somewhere, and somewhere hearts are light,
And somewhere men are laughing, and somewhere children shout;
But there is no joy in Mudville—mighty Casey has struck out.

To the Machine Tenders Union

Harry Gladstone
New York City, August 13, 1898

Harry Gladstone was a 15-year-old immigrant who organized a union for the children working in the factories. Known as "the boy agitator of the East Side," he gave this speech to a crowd of children hours before giving it to The Machine Tenders Union.

FELLOW WORKMEN, I tell you to stick together.

Think about your poor fathers and mothers you have got to support. [Think] of the schools and how you can't go there to get your education, but must spend from 14 to 15 hours a day in a pest-hole, pulling bastings, turning collars and sleeves, and running around as if you were crazy.

If you don't look out for yourselves, who will? You have not had time to grow up, to get strength for work, when you must spend your dearest days in the sweatshop. Think of the way your mothers kiss you, how they love you, and how they shed tears over you, because they see their dear boys treated like slaves.

Try to make a few dollars for them at least. Then you will come home and kiss your mamas and say "Don't cry, dear Mama. Here, I've brought you some money for rent, or for a Sabbath meal."

The only way to get the bosses to pay us good wages is to stick together, so let us be true to our union.

Science & Invention

* Benjamin Franklin (1706–1790) was an inventor, publisher, writer, statesman, scientist and philosopher. Entirely self-taught, he was also self-made, a former printer's apprentice who became one of America's founding fathers.

* By demonstrating that more than 300 products could be made from the peanut, former slave George Washington Carver (1864–1943) revolutionized the agricultural economy of the American south— freeing it from a historic dependency on cotton.

* From his New Jersey lab, Thomas Edison (1847–1931) invented many objects that shape our modern world, including the light bulb.

* Astronomer Edwin Hubble (1889–1953) discovered that our Milky Way is only one of billions of galaxies and that the universe continues to expand into infinity.

* The cotton gin, invented by Eli Whitney (1765–1825) in 1794, was a key development in America's first industrial revolution. It included a device that separated seed from cotton, and it made the South rich.

* Alexander Graham Bell (1847–1922) invented the telephone in 1876. His original name for it was an "electrical speech machine."

* Wright brothers Wilbur (1867–1912) and Orville (1871–1948)—inveterate

tinkerers and bicycle shop-owners—
were the first to successfully fly a
motorized airplane. Their history-
making flight, on December 17, 1903,
lasted 12 seconds.

✳

Albert Einstein (1879–1955)
was a Swiss patent clerk who,
in 1916, developed the ground-
breaking theory of relativity
known as "e=mc²." Awarded
the Nobel Prize in 1921, he later
emigrated to America.

✳

Michigan native Henry Ford
(1863–1947) set the course of
American industrial production
with his 1908 invention—

a motorized vehicle that could be
mass-produced. In the first 19 years,
the Ford Motor Company cranked out
approximately 10 million Model T's.

✳

Jonas Salk (1914–1995) discovered
the antidote for polio in 1954:
his vaccine, alternated with booster
shots of the vaccine developed by
Albert Sabin, effectively eradicated
the crippling disease.

✳

Samuel Morse (1791–1872)
is best known for inventing
the Morse code (1838), a dot-dot-dash
system that became indispensable
to the military.

✳

In 1975, 19-year-old Harvard dropout
Bill Gates (1955–) founded Microsoft;
Apple Computers was founded by
Steve Wozniak (1950–) and Steve
Jobs (1955–) in 1976. Together the
two companies revolutionized the
world of personal computers.

OKLAHOMA

LYRICS BY OSCAR HAMMERSTEIN II, MUSIC BY RICHARD RODGERS, 1943
(SET IN 1907)

"Brand new state!
Brand new state,
Gonna treat you great!

Gonna give you barley,
Carrots and pertaters,
Pasture fer the cattle,
Spinach and termayters!
Flowers on the prairie
Where the June bugs zoom,
Plen'y of air and plen'y of room,
Plen'y of room to swing a rope!
Plen'y of heart and plen'y of hope.

Oklahoma,
Where the wind comes sweepin' down the plain
And the wavin' wheat
Can sure smell sweet
When the wind comes right behind the rain

Oklahoma,
Ev'ry night my honey lamb and I
Sit alone and talk
And watch a hawk
Makin' lazy circles in the sky.
We know we belong to the land
And the land we belong to is grand!
And when we say
Yeeow! A-yip-i-o-ee-ay!
We're only sayin'
You're doin' fine, Oklahoma!
Oklahoma O.K.!"

AUNT MIMI'S
BLUEBERRY TOP HATS

My dear friend Nancy's Aunt Mimi made these muffins for her as a child, and now, 40 years later, everyone still thinks about them.

6 tablespoons butter

1 cup sugar

2 eggs

1 teaspoon vanilla

2 cups all-purpose flour

2 teaspoons baking powder

$^1/_2$ teaspoon salt

2 $^1/_2$ cups blueberries (not rinsed!)

$^1/_2$ cup milk

2 teaspoons sugar mixed with $^1/_2$ teaspoon cinnamon for the top

1. Preheat oven to 375° F.

2. Cream butter and sugar well. Add eggs, one at a time, and vanilla, beating well.

3. Sift and mix dry ingredients. Add to wet ingredients, alternating with milk, stirring just to blend.

4. Mash $^1/_2$ cup of berries and quickly stir into batter. Add rest of berries whole.

5. Grease muffin pan, including entire top surface. Pile batter high to make 12 large muffins. Sprinkle sugar/cinnamon on top.

6. Bake for 25–30 minutes. Let cool for 30 minutes before removing from pan.

Serves 12.

RAGTIME

E.L. DOCTOROW, 1975

(SET IN 1906)

IN 1902 FATHER BUILT A HOUSE at the crest of the Broadview Avenue hill in New Rochelle, New York. It was a three-story brown shingle with dormers, bay windows and a screened porch. Striped awnings shaded the windows. The family took possession of this stout manse on a sunny day in June and it seemed for some years thereafter that all their days would be warm and fair. The best part of Father's income was derived from the manufacture of flags and buntings and other accoutrements of patriotism, including fireworks. Patriotism was a reliable sentiment in the early 1900's. Teddy Roosevelt was President. The population customarily gathered in great numbers either out of doors for parades, public concerts, fish fries, political picnics, social outings, or indoors in meeting halls, vaudeville theatres, operas, ballrooms. There seemed to be no entertainment that did not involve great swarms of people. Trains and steamers and trolleys moved them from one place to another. That was the style, that was the way people lived. Women

were stouter then. They visited the fleet carrying white parasols. Everyone wore white in summer. Tennis racquets were hefty and the racquet faces elliptical. There was a lot of sexual fainting. There were no Negroes. There were no immigrants. On Sunday afternoon, after dinner, Father and Mother went upstairs and closed the bedroom door. Grandfather fell asleep on the divan in the parlor. The Little Boy in the sailor blouse sat on the screened porch and waved away the flies. Down at the bottom of the hill Mother's Younger Brother boarded the streetcar and rode to the end of the line. He was a lonely, withdrawn young man with blond moustaches, and was thought to be having difficulty finding himself. The end of the line was an empty field of tall marsh grasses. The air was salt. Mother's Younger Brother in his white linen suit and boater rolled his trousers and walked barefoot in the salt marshes. Sea birds started and flew up. This was the time in our history when Winslow Homer was doing his painting. A certain light was still available along the Eastern seaboard. Homer painted the light. It gave the sea a heavy dull menace and shone coldly on the rocks and shoals of the New England coast. There were unexplained shipwrecks and brave towline rescues. Odd things went on in lighthouses and in

Ragtime

shacks nestled in the wild beach plum. Across America sex and
death were barely distinguishable. Runaway women died in the rigors
of ecstasy. Stories were hushed up and reporters paid off by rich
families. One read between the lines of the journals and gazettes. In
New York City the papers were full of the shooting of the famous
architect Stanford White by Harry K. Thaw, eccentric scion of a
coke and railroad fortune. Harry K. Thaw was the husband of
Evelyn Nesbit, the celebrated beauty who had once been Stanford
White's mistress. The shooting took place in the roof garden of the
Madison Square Garden on 26th Street, a spectacular block-long
building of yellow brick and terra cotta that White himself had
designed in the Sevillian style. It was the opening night of a revue
entitled *Mamzelle Champagne*, and as the chorus sang and danced
the eccentric scion wearing on this summer night a straw boater
and heavy black coat pulled out a pistol and shot the famous architect three times in the head. On the roof. There were screams.
Evelyn fainted. She had been a well-known artist's model at the age
of fifteen. Her underclothes were white. Her husband habitually
whipped her. She happened once to meet Emma Goldman, the
revolutionary. Goldman lashed her with her tongue. Apparently

RAGTIME

there *were* Negroes. There *were* immigrants. And though the newspapers called the shooting the Crime of the Century, Goldman knew it was only 1906 and there were ninety-four years to go.

Mother's Younger Bother was in love with Evelyn Nesbit. He had closely followed the scandal surrounding her name and had begun to reason that the death of her lover Stanford White and the imprisonment of her husband Harry K. Thaw left her in need of the attentions of a genteel middle-class young man with no money. He thought about her all the time. He was desperate to have her. In his room pinned on the wall was a newspaper drawing by Charles Dana Gibson entitled "The Eternal Question." It showed Evelyn in profile, with a profusion of hair, one thick strand undone and fallen in the configuration of a question mark. Her downcast eye was embellished with a fallen ringlet that threw her brow in shadow. Her nose was delicately upturned. Her mouth was slightly pouted. Her long neck curved like a bird taking wing. Evelyn Nesbit had caused the death of one man and wrecked the life of another and from that he deduced that there was nothing in life worth having, worth wanting, but the embrace of her thin arms.

RAGTIME

The afternoon was a blue haze. Tidewater seeped into his foot-prints. He bent down and found a perfect shell specimen, a variety not common to western Long Island Sound. It was a voluted pink and amber shell the shape of a thimble, and what he did in the hazy sun with the salt drying on his ankles was to throw his head back and drink the minute amount of sea water in the shell. Gulls wheeled overhead, crying like oboes, and behind him at the land end of the marsh, out of sight behind the tall grasses, the distant bell of the North Avenue streetcar tolled its warning.

Across town the little boy in the sailor suit was suddenly restless and began to measure the length of the porch. He trod with his toe upon the runner of the cane-backed rocking chair. He had reached that age of knowledge and wisdom in a child when it is not expected by the adults around him and consequently goes unrecognized. He read the newspaper daily and was currently following the dispute between the professional baseballers and a scientist who claimed that the curve ball was an optical illusion. He felt that the circum-stances of his family's life operated against his need to see things and to go places. For instance he had conceived an enormous interest in

Ragtime

the works and career of Harry Houdini, the escape artist. But he had not been taken to a performance. Houdini was a headliner in the top vaudeville circuits. His audiences were poor people—carriers, peddlers, policemen, children. His life was absurd. He went all over the world accepting all kinds of bondage and escaping. He was roped to a chair. He escaped. He was chained to a ladder. He escaped. He was handcuffed, his legs were put in irons, he was tied up in a strait jacket and put in a locked cabinet. He escaped. He escaped from bank vaults, nailed-up barrels, sewn mailbags; he escaped from a zinc-lined Knabe piano case, a giant football, a galvanized iron boiler, a rolltop desk, a sausage skin. His escapes were mystifying because he never damaged or appeared to unlock what he escaped from. The screen was pulled away and there he stood disheveled but triumphant beside the inviolate container that was supposed to have contained him. He waved to the crowd. He escaped from a sealed milk can filled with water. He escaped from a Siberian exile van. From a Chinese torture crucifix. From a Hamburg penitentiary. From an English prison ship. From a Boston jail. He was chained to automobile tires, water wheels, cannon, and escaped. He dove manacled from a bridge into the

Ragtime

Mississippi, the Seine, the Mersey, and came up waving. He hung upside down and strait-jacketed from cranes, biplanes and the tops of buildings. He was dropped into the ocean padlocked in a diving suit fully weighted and not connected to an air supply, and he escaped. He was buried alive in a grave and could not escape, and had to be rescued. Hurriedly, they dug him out. The earth is too heavy, he said gasping. His nails bled. Soil fell from his eyes. He was drained of color and couldn't stand. His assistant threw up. Houdini wheezed and sputtered. He coughed blood. They cleaned him off and took him back to the hotel. Today, nearly fifty years since his death, the audience for escapes is even larger.

The little boy stood at the end of the porch and fixed his gaze on a bluebottle fly traversing the screen in a way that made it appear to be coming up the hill from North Avenue. The fly flew off. An automobile was coming up the hill from North Avenue. As it drew closer he saw it was a black 45-horsepower Pope-Toledo Runabout. He ran along the porch and stood at the top of the steps. The car came past his house, made a loud noise and swerved into the telephone pole. The little boy ran inside and called upstairs to his mother and father. Grandfather woke with a start. The boy ran back to the

Ragtime

porch. The driver and the passenger were standing in the street looking at the car: it had big wheels with pneumatic tires and wooden spokes painted in black enamel. It had brass headlamps in front of the radiator and brass sidelamps over the fenders. It had tufted upholstery and double side entrances. It did not appear to be damaged. The driver was in livery. He folded back the hood and a geyser of white steam shot up with a hiss.

A number of people looked on from their front yards. But Father, adjusting the chain on his vest, went down to the sidewalk to see if there was something he could do. The car's owner was Harry Houdini, the famous escape artist. He was spending the day driving thought Westchester. He was thinking of buying some property. He was invited into the house while the radiator cooled. He surprised them with his modest, almost colorless demeanor. He seemed depressed. His success had brought into vaudeville a host of competitors. Consequently he had to think of more and more dangerous escapes. He was a short, powerfully built man, an athlete obviously, with strong hands and with back and arm muscles that suggested themselves through the cut of his rumpled tweed suit which, though well tailored, was worn this day inappropriately.

Ragtime

The thermometer read in the high eighties. Houdini had unruly stiff hair parted in the middle and clear blue eyes, which did not stop moving. He was very respectful to Mother and Father and spoke of his profession with diffidence. This struck them as appropriate. The little boy stared at him. Mother had ordered lemonade. It was brought into the parlor and Houdini drank it gratefully. The room was kept cool by the awnings on the windows. The windows themselves were shut to keep out the heat. Houdini wanted to undo his collar. He felt trapped by the heavy square furnishings, the drapes and dark rugs, the Oriental silk cushions, the green glass lampshades. There was a chaise with a zebra rug. Noticing Houdini's gaze Father mentioned that he had shot that zebra on a hunting trip in Africa. Father was an amateur explorer of considerable reputation. He was past president of the New York Explorers Club to which he made an annual disbursement. In fact in just a few days he would be leaving to carry the Club's standard on the third Peary expedition to the Arctic. You mean, Houdini said, you're going with Peary to the Pole? God willing, Father replied. He sat back in his chair and lit a cigar. Houdini became voluble. He paced back and forth. He spoke of his own travels, his tours of Europe. But the Pole! he said.

RAGTIME

Now that's something. You must be pretty good to get picked for that. He turned his blue eyes on Mother. And keeping the home fires burning ain't so easy either, he said. He was not without charm. He smiled and Mother, a large blond woman, lowered her eyes. Houdini then spent a few minutes doing small deft tricks with objects at hand for the little boy. When he took his leave the entire family saw him to the door. Father and Grandfather shook his hand. Houdini walked down the path that ran under the big maple tree and then descended the stone steps that led to the street. The chauffeur was waiting, the car was parked correctly. Houdini climbed in the seat next to the driver and waved. People stood looking on from their yards. The little boy had followed the magician to the street and now stood at the front of the Pope-Toledo gazing at the distorted macrocephalic image of himself in the shiny brass fitting of the headlight. Houdini thought the boy comely, fair like his mother, and tow-headed, but a little soft-looking. He leaned over the side door. Goodbye, Sonny, he said holding out his hand. Warn the Duke, the little boy said. Then he ran off.

ALEXANDRA DREW HER SHAWL CLOSER about her and stood leaning against the frame of the mill, looking at the stars which glittered so keenly through the frosty autumn air. She always loved to watch them, to think of their vastness and distance, and of their ordered march. It fortified her to reflect upon the great operations of nature, and when she thought of the law that lay behind them, she felt a sense of personal security. That night she had a new consciousness of the country, felt almost a new relation to it. Even her talk with the boys had not taken away the feeling that had overwhelmed her when she drove back to the Divide that afternoon. She had never known before how much the country meant to her. The chirping of the insects down in the long grass had been like the sweetest music. She had felt as if her heart were hiding down there, somewhere, with the quail and the plover and all the little wild things that crooned or buzzed in the sun. Under the long shaggy ridges, she felt the future stirring.

AMERICA THE BEAUTIFUL

KATHARINE LEE BATES. 1913

O beautiful for spacious skies,
    For amber waves of grain,
For purple mountain majesties
    Above the fruited plain!
America! America!
    God shed His grace on thee
And crown thy good with brotherhood
    From sea to shining sea!

O beautiful for pilgrim feet,
    Whose stern, impassioned stress
A thoroughfare for freedom beat
    Across the wilderness!
America! America!
    God mend thine every flaw,
Confirm thy soul in self-control,
    Thy liberty in law!

O beautiful for heroes proved
    In liberating strife,
Who more than self their country loved,
    And mercy more than life!
America! America!
    May God thy gold refine,
Till all success be nobleness
    And every grain divine!

O beautiful for patriot dream
    That sees beyond the years
Thine alabaster cities gleam
    Undimmed by human tears!
America! America!
    God shed His grace on thee,
And crown thy good with brotherhood
    From sea to shining sea!

191

World War I

In 1914, tensions already building in Europe came to a head when Archduke Francis Ferdinand of Austria-Hungary was assassinated in Sarajevo by a Serb nationalist. A month later, the world was at war.

America's declared stance of neutrality was severely strained after German subs torpedoed the passenger ship *Lusitania* on May 1, 1915, killing over a thousand people, 123 of them Americans. The tide of public opinion was irreversibly shifted.

Forsaking its own policy of isolationism, America declared war on Germany on April 6, 1917, three years after the war began. The war ended less than a year later.

When the war began, the American air force had just 12 officers, 54 enlisted men and fewer than a dozen planes.

13,000 women (known as Yeomanettes) served with the Navy and Marine Corps in WWI, with the same status as men.

Writers Ernest Hemingway, John Dos Passos, e.e. cummings, W. Somerset Maugham and Dashiell Hammett all served as ambulance drivers during WWI. Gertrude Stein also volunteered medical assistance.

Mustard gas, named for its color and odor, was used later in the war; a blistering agent, it acted with severity on any exposed, moist skin.

WWI innovations—such as trench warfare, tanks and airplanes—changed the way war was fought. Instead of the isolated battles of the past, war was waged on fronts that stretched for miles.

⋆

Other WWI inventions included poison gas, first used by the Germans on April 22, 1915, in France. The ensuing five-mile cloud, composed of 168 tons of chlorine gas, resulted in widespread panic and death.

⋆

The war's end came at the low point of German resources and morale. Woodrow Wilson's Fourteen Points were accepted as general terms for Germany's surrender on November 11, 1918.

⋆

More than 9 million soldiers died in the war. 117,000 of them were Americans.

⋆

Best known for having led the first U.S. troops into France, General John Joseph Pershing (1860–1948) held degrees from a teaching academy, West Point and the University of Nebraska's law school. Among his military innovations was the National Guard.

⋆

Some 750 poets, playwrights, writers, artists, architects and composers were killed in WWI.

THE ROAD NOT TAKEN

ROBERT FROST, 1916

TWO ROADS DIVERGED IN A YELLOW WOOD,
AND SORRY I COULD NOT TRAVEL BOTH
AND BE ONE TRAVELER, LONG I STOOD
AND LOOKED DOWN ONE AS FAR AS I COULD
TO WHERE IT BENT IN THE UNDERGROWTH;

THEN TOOK THE OTHER, AS JUST AS FAIR,
AND HAVING PERHAPS THE BETTER CLAIM,
BECAUSE IT WAS GRASSY AND WANTED WEAR;
THOUGH AS FOR THAT, THE PASSING THERE
HAD WORN THEM REALLY ABOUT THE SAME,

AND BOTH THAT MORNING EQUALLY LAY
IN LEAVES NO STEP HAD TRODDEN BLACK.
OH, I KEPT THE FIRST FOR ANOTHER DAY!
YET KNOWING HOW WAY LEADS ON TO WAY,
I DOUBTED IF I SHOULD EVER COME BACK.

I SHALL BE TELLING THIS WITH A SIGH
SOMEWHERE AGES AND AGES HENCE:
TWO ROADS DIVERGED IN A WOOD, AND I—
I TOOK THE ONE LESS TRAVELED BY,
AND THAT HAS MADE ALL THE DIFFERENCE.

MEATLOAF WITH GRAVY
AND MASHED POTATOES

Meatloaf has been an American staple since the early 1900s. I have been looking for a great recipe for it most of my life. This is it.

Meatloaf

2 pounds ground round

$^1/_2$ cup yellow onions, diced

2 tablespoons parsley, finely chopped

1 $^1/_2$ tablespoons Worcestershire sauce

1 egg

$^1/_2$ can cream of mushroom soup

1 clove garlic, finely chopped

1 teaspoon salt-free seasoning (like Mrs. Dash Table Blend or Trader Joe's 21 Seasoning Salute)

5 ounces Monterey Jack cheese, divided in half

$^1/_4$ cup ketchup

4 bacon slices

$^1/_4$ cup red wine

Gravy

1 to 2 tablespoons flour

$^1/_4$ cup beef broth

$^1/_2$ can cream of mushroom soup

$^1/_4$ teaspoon sea salt

1. Preheat oven to 350°F.

2. In a large bowl, mix the meat, onions, parsley, Worcestershire sauce, egg, mushroom soup, garlic and seasoning together with your hands.

3. Press the mixture into a flattened circle. Put the two hunks of cheese in the center of the circle and fold the meat into a loaf shape to cover them. Transfer into a medium-size casserole dish so that the meatloaf sits in the middle with room on the sides.

4. Cover the top of the meat with ketchup, lay the bacon strips on top, and pour wine into the bottom of the dish.

5. Bake uncovered for 1 hour. Drain the drippings into a saucepan, return the meatloaf to the oven and broil for 5 minutes, until the bacon is sizzling.

6. While the meatloaf broils, heat the drippings over a medium flame, whisking in as much flour as there are drippings. When the gravy bubbles, whisk in the broth and mushroom soup. Continue stirring until thick (approximately 5 minutes). Season to taste and serve.

Mashed Potatoes

6 baking potatoes, peeled and halved

¹/₂ cup milk

¹/₄ cup heavy cream

1 stick unsalted butter

4 tablespoons chopped parsley

salt and freshly ground pepper to taste

1. Place potatoes in enough lightly salted cold water to cover them. Bring to a boil and cook approximately 15 minutes.

2. Drain when the potatoes are soft.

3. Scald the milk and cream in a medium-size saucepan. Add butter and continue cooking on low heat until melted.

4. Mash the potatoes in their pot. Place over medium heat and gradually pour in the scalded milk, stirring with a wooden spoon. Mix until smooth and creamy.

7. Fold in herbs and seasonings.

Serves 4 to 6.

OVER THERE

GEORGE M. COHAN, 1917

Johnnie, get your gun, get your gun, get your gun,
Take it on the run, on the run, on the run;
Hear them calling you and me,
Ev'ry son of liberty.
Hurry right away, no delay, go today.
Make your Daddy glad
To have had such a lad.
Tell your sweetheart not to pine,
To be proud her boy's in line.

Chorus
Over there, over there,
Send the word, send the word, over there,
That the Yanks are coming, the Yanks are coming,
The drums rum-tumming everywhere
So prepare, say a pray'r,

Send the word, send the word to beware,
We'll be over, we're coming over,
And we won't come back til it's
      over over there.
Over there.

Johnnie, get your gun, get your gun, get your gun,
Johnnie show the Hun, you're a son of a gun!
Hoist the flag and let her fly,
Like true heroes do or die
Pack your little kit, show your grit, do your bit,
Soldiers to the ranks from the towns and the tanks
Make your mother proud of you,
And to liberty be true.

(Chorus)

FROM
RENASCENCE

EDNA ST. VINCENT MILLAY, 1917

ALL I COULD SEE FROM WHERE I STOOD
WAS THREE LONG MOUNTAINS AND A WOOD;
I TURNED AND LOOKED ANOTHER WAY,
AND SAW THREE ISLANDS IN A BAY.
SO WITH MY EYES I TRACED THE LINE
OF THE HORIZON, THIN AND FINE,
STRAIGHT AROUND TILL I WAS COME
BACK TO WHERE I'D STARTED FROM;
AND ALL I SAW FROM WHERE I STOOD
WAS THREE LONG MOUNTAINS AND A WOOD.

OVER THESE THINGS I COULD NOT SEE:
THESE WERE THE THINGS THAT BOUNDED ME.
AND I COULD TOUCH THEM WITH MY HAND,
ALMOST, I THOUGHT, FROM WHERE I STAND.

AND ALL AT ONCE THINGS SEEMED SO SMALL
MY BREATH CAME SHORT, AND SCARCE AT ALL.
BUT, SURE, THE SKY IS BIG, I SAID:
MILES AND MILES ABOVE MY HEAD;
SO HERE UPON MY BACK I'LL LIE
AND LOOK MY FILL INTO THE SKY.
AND SO I LOOKED, AND AFTER ALL,
THE SKY WAS NOT SO VERY TALL.
THE SKY, I SAID, MUST SOMEWHERE STOP.
AND—SURE ENOUGH!—I SEE THE TOP!
THE SKY, I THOUGHT, IS NOT SO GRAND;
I'MOST COULD TOUCH IT WITH MY HAND!
AND REACHING UP MY HAND TO TRY,
I SCREAMED TO FEEL IT TOUCH THE SKY.

THE NEGRO SPEAKS OF RIVERS

LANGSTON HUGHES, 1921

I've known rivers:
I've known rivers ancient as the world and older than
    the flow of human blood in human veins.

My soul has grown deep like the rivers.

I bathed in the Euphrates when dawns were young.
I built my hut near the Congo and it lulled me to sleep.
I looked upon the Nile and raised the pyramids above it.
I heard the singing of the Mississippi when Abe Lincoln
    went down to New Orleans, and I've seen its
    muddy bosom turn all golden in the sunset.

I've known rivers:
Ancient, dusky rivers.

My soul has grown deep like the rivers.

California

The California Gold Rush began on January 24, 1848, when gold was accidentally discovered at Sutter's Mill, on the South Fork of the American River in Coloma, near Sacramento.

More people live in California than in any other state in the U.S. In 2001, there were more than 34 million.

The "Eternal God" is a 12,000-year-old redwood tree in the Prairie Creek Redwoods State Park. It's the oldest living thing on the planet, but at 238 feet tall it isn't the biggest tree. That title belongs to a giant sequoia called "General Sherman" in Sequoia National Park, which tops out at 275 feet and measures more than 102 feet around.

Some San Francisco originals: blue jeans and fortune cookies.

The San Andreas fault line runs 650 miles up the California coast, marking the collision of the Pacific and North American tectonic plates. Thousands of small earthquakes occur in California every year; historically, a major quake has hit the southern region every 150 years. The last big one hit in 1857.

Hollywood began in 1908, when a few independent New York filmmakers moved west to set up shop. The town's first full-length motion picture was filmed in 1915.

East finally met west in 1869, when the Central Pacific and Union Pacific railroads were connected.

The hottest day ever in America was in California's Death Valley on July 10, 1913. It was a sweltering 135°F!

Hewlett-Packard was the first tech company in Silicon Valley. In 1938, Stanford University engineers Bill Hewlett and Dave Packard started it in a garage with $1,538.

Los Angeles is moving eastward at an estimated rate of one-fifth of an inch per year.

Mel Blanc, the voice behind Bugs Bunny and Porky Pig, is buried in Hollywood Memorial Park. His headstone reads, "That's all, folks!"

Each October, Pacific Grove, California, becomes home to thousands of Monarch butterflies, who travel up to 2,000 miles to winter and mate there. It's been a misdemeanor to harm a Monarch in Pacific Grove since 1939.

California's stint as a republic, after declaring freedom from Mexico on June 14, 1846, lasted one month. It then spent four years as a U.S. territory before officially becoming a state on September 9, 1850.

THE PLEDGE OF ALLEGIANCE

OFFICIALLY ADOPTED ON FLAG DAY, JUNE 14 1924
("UNDER GOD" AMENDMENT MADE BY CONGRESS IN 1954)

I pledge allegiance to the flag
of the United States of America
and to the republic for which it stands;
one nation under God, indivisible,
with liberty and justice for all.

CALIFORNIA, HERE I COME

AL JOLSON, B.G. DESYLVA AND JOSEPH MEYER, 1924

California, Here I Come,
Right back where I started from.
Where bowers of flowers bloom in the sun.
Each morning at dawning birdies sing and ev'rything.
A sunkissed miss said, "Don't be late."
That's why I can hardly wait.
Open up that golden gate;
California, Here I Come!

State Capitals

UNITE OR DIE

Olympia ✪ WASHINGTON

Salem ✪

OREGON

Helena ✪ MONTANA

Boise ✪ IDAHO

WYOMING

NEVADA

✪ Salt Lake City Cheyenr

Sacramento ✪ ✪ Carson City

Denver

CALIFORNIA

UTAH

COLOR/

Santa Fe ✪

ARIZONA

ALASKA

Phoenix ✪ NEW MEXIC

Juneau ✪

Honolulu ✪

HAWAII

TH DAKOTA
✪ Bismarck

MINNESOTA

MICHIGAN

MAINE

Montpelier ✪
NEW
HAMPSHIRE

✪ Augusta

Concord

TH DAKOTA
✪ Pierre

St. Paul ✪

WISCONSIN

✪ Lansing

VERMONT

Albany
✪

✪ Boston
MASSACHUSETTS
✪ Providence

NEW YORK

RHODE ISLAND

Madison ✪

Hartford
✪

CONNECTICUT

IOWA

PENNSYLVANIA

Trenton
✪

NEBRASKA

✪ Des Moines

Harrisburg
✪

NEW
JERSEY

OHIO

✪ Lincoln

ILLINOIS

INDIANA

Columbus
✪

MARYLAND

Dover
✪

DELAWARE

Annapolis
✪

Springfield ✪
Indianapolis ✪

WEST
VIRGINIA

✪ Richmond

Topeka ✪

Jefferson City ✪
Frankfort

Charleston
✪

KANSAS

MISSOURI

KENTUCKY

VIRGINIA

✪ Raleigh

Nashville ✪

NORTH
CAROLINA

OKLAHOMA

TENNESSEE

Oklahoma City ✪

ARKANSAS

Columbia
✪

Little Rock ✪

✪ Atlanta

SOUTH
CAROLINA

ALABAMA

GEORGIA

MISSISSIPPI

TEXAS

Jackson ✪

Montgomery ✪

LOUISIANA

✪ Tallahassee

✪ Austin

✪ Baton Rouge

FLORIDA

215

FROM

THE GREAT GATSBY

F. SCOTT FITZGERALD, 1925

OVER THE GREAT BRIDGE, with the sunlight through the girders making a constant flicker upon the moving cars, with the city rising up across the river in white heaps and sugar lumps all built with a wish out of non-olfactory money. The city seen from the Queensboro Bridge is always the city seen for the first time, in its first wild promise of all the mystery and the beauty in the world.

THANKSGIVING DINNER

(TURKEY, STUFFING, GRAVY, GLAZED CARROTS AND CARMELIZED ONIONS)

Turkey, Stuffing and Gravy

1 large bag (14 ounces) Pepperidge Farm Country Style or Herb Seasoned stuffing

¼ cup Italian parsley, minced

2 onions, minced

1 cup chopped walnuts or chestnuts

1 turkey (approximately 14 pounds)

2 lemons with the skin sliced off

1 stick butter

5 cups chicken stock

1 tablespoon white flour

1 teaspoon cornstarch

The first Thanksgiving dinner was in 1621, when Pilgrims invited more than 90 Native Americans to a three-day feast, which included wild turkey and venison. Today the tradition revolves around the turkey. Everybody has a trick for producing the perfect bird. Mine is simple: baste every 15–20 minutes and bake at a relatively low heat—that way you can cook it until it starts to sag and it will never be dry. Add our mashed potatoes to these side dishes, and you're all set!

1. Preheat oven to 450° F.

2. Prepare the stuffing according to package instructions. Add parsley, onions and nuts.

3. Remove gizzard, livers, neck, and anything else in the turkey cavity. Rinse and dry turkey, and rub inside and out with lemons.

4. Slice the stick of butter into thin pieces and place all over the outside of the turkey. Stuff the turkey.

5. Put the turkey into a roasting pan and pour chicken stock around it. Put into the oven and bake for 20 minutes.

6. Turn heat down to 375° F and baste every 15 minutes for just under five hours (20 minutes per pound). If it gets too brown, cover loosely with aluminum foil.

7. Remove the turkey from the oven and let it cool for 20 minutes.

8. Remove as much fat as possible from the pan. Pour $1/2$ cup of the remaining liquid from the turkey pan into a saucepan. Mix in the flour and cornstarch. When smooth, place saucepan on medium heat and stir until thickened.

9. Remove the stuffing from the turkey and carve.

Glazed Carrots

10–12 medium carrots

4 tablespoons butter

1 $1/2$ tablespoons sugar

salt and pepper to taste

1. Peel, trim and dice the carrots.

2. Simmer the carrots in a pot of salted boiling water until tender, and drain.

3. Melt the butter in a skillet over medium heat. Add the sugar and stir until dissolved.

4. Add the carrots and toss in the butter and sugar until thoroughly coated. Season with salt and pepper and cook until heated through.

Caramelized Onions

3 pints pearl onions

6 tablespoons butter

3 tablespoons sugar

1. Peel the onions and place them in a pot of salted boiling water. Simmer until tender, and drain.

2. Melt the butter in a skillet over medium heat. Add the onions, shaking the pan to coat the onions with butter.

3. Sprinkle with sugar and cook until the sugar begins to caramelize. When the onions are brown, serve.

Serves 6 to 8.

"HOPE" IS THE THING WITH FEATHERS

EMILY DICKINSON, 1929

"HOPE" IS THE THING WITH FEATHERS—
THAT PERCHES IN THE SOUL—
AND SINGS THE TUNE WITHOUT THE WORDS—
AND NEVER STOPS—AT ALL—

AND SWEETEST—IN THE GALE—IS HEARD—
AND SORE MUST BE THE STORM—
THAT COULD ABASH THE LITTLE BIRD
THAT KEPT SO MANY WARM—

I'VE HEARD IT IN THE CHILLEST LAND—
AND ON THE STRANGEST SEA—
YET, NEVER, IN EXTREMITY,
IT ASKED A CRUMB—OF ME.

"THE ONLY THING WE HAVE TO FEAR IS FEAR ITSELF"

FRANKLIN DELANO ROOSEVELT
WASHINGTON, D. C., MARCH 4, 1933

In his inaugural address to a nation still reeling from the Great Depression, Franklin Delano Roosevelt conveyed a bold sense of hope and a steely resolve.

THIS IS A DAY OF NATIONAL CONSECRATION, and I am certain that my fellow-Americans expect that on my induction into the Presidency I will address them with a candor and a decision which the present situation of our nation impels.

This is preeminently the time to speak the truth, the whole truth, frankly and boldly. Nor need we shrink from honestly facing conditions in our country today. This great nation will endure as it has endured, will revive and will prosper.

So first of all let me assert my firm belief that the only thing we have to fear is fear itself—nameless, unreasoning, unjustified terror which paralyzes needed efforts to convert retreat into advance.

In every dark hour of our national life a leadership of frankness and vigor has met with that understanding and support of the people themselves which is essential to victory. I am convinced that you will again give that support to leadership in these critical days.

In such a spirit on my part and on yours we face our common difficulties. They concern, thank God, only material things. Values have shrunken to fantastic levels; taxes have risen; our ability to pay has fallen; government of all kinds is faced by serious curtailment of income; the means of exchange are frozen in the currents of trade; the withered leaves of industrial enterprise lie on every side; farmers find no markets for their produce; the savings of many years in thousands of families are gone.

More important, a host of unemployed citizens face the grim problem of existence, and an equally great number toil with little return. Only a foolish optimist can deny the dark realities of the moment.

Yet our distress comes from no failure of substance. We are stricken by no plague of locusts. Compared with the perils which our forefathers conquered because they believed and were not afraid, we have still much to be thankful for. Nature still offers her bounty and human efforts have multiplied it. Plenty is at our doorstep, but a generous use of it languishes in the very sight of the supply.

Our greatest primary task is to put people to work. This is no unsolvable problem if we face it wisely and courageously.

It can be accomplished in part by direct recruiting by the government itself, treating the task as we would treat the emergency of a war, but at the same time, through this employment, accomplishing greatly needed projects to stimulate and reorganize the use of our natural resources....

Finally, in our progress toward a resumption of work we require two safeguards against a return of the evils of the old order; there must be a strict supervision of all banking and credits and investments; there must be an end to speculation with other people's money, and there must be provision for an adequate but sound currency....

We do not distrust the future of essential democracy. The people of the United States have not failed. In their need they have registered a mandate that they want direct, vigorous action.

They have asked for discipline and direction under leadership. They have made me the present instrument of their wishes. In the spirit of the gift I take it.

In this dedication of a nation we humbly ask the blessing of God. May He protect each and every one of us! May He guide me in the days to come!

SUMMERTIME

GEORGE GERSHWIN, DUBOSE HEYWARD AND IRA GERSHWIN, 1935

Summertime and the livin' is easy,
Fish are jumpin' and the cotton is high.
Oh, your daddy's rich, and your ma is good lookin,'
So hush, little baby, don' you cry.

One of these mornin's you goin' to rise up singin,'
Then you'll spread yo' wings an' you'll take the sky.
But till that mornin,' there's a-nothin' can harm you
With Daddy and Mammy standin' by.

To Kill a Mockingbird

Harper Lee, 1960 (set in the 1930s)

When he was nearly thirteen, my brother Jem got his arm badly broken at the elbow. When it healed, and Jem's fears of never being able to play football were assuaged, he was seldom self-conscious about his injury. His left arm was somewhat shorter than his right; when he stood or walked, the back of his hand was at right angles to his body, his thumb parallel to his thigh. He couldn't have cared less, so long as he could pass and punt.

When enough years had gone by to enable us to look back on them, we sometimes discussed the events leading to his accident. I maintain that the Ewells started it all, but Jem, who was four years my senior, said it began the summer Dill came to us, when Dill first gave us the idea of making Boo Radley come out.

I said if he wanted to take a broad view of the thing, it really began with Andrew Jackson. If General Jackson hadn't run the Creeks up the creek, Simon Finch would never have paddled up the

To Kill a Mockingbird

Alabama, and where would we be if he hadn't? We were far too old to settle an argument with a fist-fight, so we consulted Atticus. Our father said we were both right.

Being Southerners, it was a source of shame to some members of the family that we had no recorded ancestors on either side of the Battle of Hastings. All we had was Simon Finch, a fur-trapping apothecary from Cornwall whose piety was exceeded only by his stinginess. In England, Simon was irritated by the persecution of those who called themselves Methodists at the hands of their more liberal brethren, and as Simon called himself a Methodist, he worked his way across the Atlantic to Philadelphia, thence to Mobile, and up the Saint Stephens. Mindful of John Wesley's strictures on the use of many words in buying and selling, Simon made a pile practicing medicine, but in this pursuit he was unhappy lest he be tempted into doing what he knew was not for the glory of God, as the putting on of gold and costly apparel. So Simon, having forgotten his teacher's dictum on the possession of human chattels, bought three slaves and with their aid established a homestead on the banks of the Alabama River some forty miles above Saint

To Kill a Mockingbird

Stephens. He returned to Saint Stephens only once, to find a wife, and with her established a line that ran high to daughters. Simon lived to an impressive age and died rich.

It was customary for the men in the family to remain on Simon's homestead, Finch's Landing, and make their living from cotton. The place was self-sufficient: modest in comparison with the empires around it, the Landing nevertheless produced everything required to sustain life except ice, wheat flour, and articles of clothing, supplied by river-boats from Mobile.

Simon would have regarded with impotent fury the disturbance between the North and the South, as it left his descendants stripped of everything but their land, yet the tradition of living on the land remained unbroken until well into the twentieth century, when my father, Atticus Finch, went to Montgomery to read law, and his younger brother went to Boston to study medicine. Their sister Alexandra was the Finch who remained at the Landing: she married a taciturn man who spent most of his time lying in a hammock by the river wondering if his trout-lines were full.

TO KILL A MOCKINGBIRD

When my father was admitted to the bar, he returned to Maycomb and began his practice. Maycomb, some twenty miles east of Finch's Landing, was the county seat of Maycomb County. Atticus's office in the courthouse contained little more than a hat rack, a spittoon, a checkerboard and an unsullied Code of Alabama. His first two clients were the last two persons hanged in the Maycomb jail. Atticus had urged them to accept the state's generosity in allowing them to plead Guilty to second-degree murder and escape with their lives, but they were Haverfords, in Maycomb County a name synonymous with jackass. The Haverfords had dispatched Maycomb's leading blacksmith in a misunderstanding arising from the alleged wrongful detention of a mare, were imprudent enough to do it in the presence of three witnesses, and insisted that the-son-of-a-bitch-had-it-coming-to-him was a good enough defense for anybody. They persisted in pleading Not Guilty to first-degree murder, so there was nothing much Atticus could do for his clients except be present for their departure, an occasion that was probably the beginning of my father's profound distaste for the practice of criminal law.

To Kill a Mockingbird

    During his first five years in Maycomb, Atticus practiced economy more than anything; for several years thereafter he invested his earnings in his brother's education. John Hale Finch was ten years younger than my father, and chose medicine at a time when cotton was not worth growing; but after getting Uncle Jack started, Atticus derived a reasonable income from the law. He liked Maycomb, he was Maycomb County born and bred; he knew his people, they knew him, and because of Simon Finch's industry, Atticus was related by blood or marriage to nearly every family in the town.

    Maycomb was an old town, but it was a tired old town when I first knew it. In rainy weather the streets turned to red slop; grass grew on the sidewalks, the courthouse sagged in the square. Somehow, it was hotter then: a black dog suffered on a summer's day; bony mules hitched to Hoover carts flicked flies in the sweltering shade of the live oaks on the square. Men's stiff collars wilted by nine in the morning. Ladies bathed before noon, after their three-o'clock naps, and by nightfall were like soft teacakes with frostings of sweat and sweet talcum.

To Kill a Mockingbird

People moved slowly then. They ambled across the square, shuffled in and out of the stores around it, took their time about everything. A day was twenty-four hours long but seemed longer. There was no hurry, for there was nowhere to go, nothing to buy and no money to buy it with, nothing to see outside the boundaries of Maycomb County. But it was a time of vague optimism for some of the people: Maycomb County had recently been told that it had nothing to fear but fear itself.

We lived on the main residential street in town—Atticus, Jem and I, plus Calpurnia our cook. Jem and I found our father satisfactory: he played with us, read to us, and treated us with courteous detachment.

Calpurnia was something else again. She was all angles and bones; she was nearsighted; she squinted; her hand was wide as a bed slat and twice as hard. She was always ordering me out of the kitchen, asking me why I couldn't behave as well as Jem when she knew he was older, and calling me home when I wasn't ready to come. Our battles were epic and one-sided. Calpurnia always won, mainly because Atticus always took her side. She had been with us ever since Jem was born, and I had felt her tyrannical presence as long as I could remember.

Our mother died when I was two, so I never felt her absence. She was a Graham from Montgomery; Atticus met her when he was first elected to the state legislature. He was middle-aged then, she was fifteen years his junior. Jem was the product of their first year of marriage; four years later I was born, and two years later our mother died from a sudden heart attack. They said it ran in her family. I did not miss her, but I think Jem did. He remembered her clearly, and sometimes in the middle of a game he would sigh at length, then go off and play by himself behind the carhouse. When he was like that, I knew better than to bother him.

When I was six and Jem was nearly ten, our summertime boundaries (within calling distance of Calpurnia) were Mrs. Henry Lafayette Dubose's house two doors to the north of us, and the Radley Place three doors to the south. We were never tempted to break them. The Radley Place was inhabited by an unknown entity the mere description of whom was enough to make us behave for days on end; Mrs. Dubose was plain hell.

That was the summer we met Dill.

The West

90% of North Dakota is covered with farms, making it America's most rural state.

✳

South Dakota's electoral votes have only gone to the Democratic candidate in four presidential elections.

✳

At the juncture of Colorado, New Mexico, Arizona and Utah, known as the Four Corners, you can literally touch four states at once— one with each limb.

✳

Montana's Roe River is the shortest river in the world, flowing 200 feet between Giant Springs and the Missouri River near Great Falls.

✳

Browning, Montana holds the record for the biggest 24-hour temperature change: on January 23, 1916, the mercury plunged 100 degrees—from 44°F to -56°F.

THROWING THE LASSO

Denver, Colorado has an average of 300 days of sunshine a year—more than Miami.

Oregon produces more peppermint, blackberries, boysenberries, black raspberries and hazelnuts than any other state.

Lake Tahoe, which straddles California and Nevada, is 1,645 feet deep. Sitting high in the Sierra Nevada range, it is the deepest and largest mountain lake in North America.

Wyoming's Wind River Reservation is home to some 21,000 Arapaho and Shoshone Indians, and covers more than 2.2 million acres. It's the third-largest reservation in the U.S.

Mormons comprise 70% of Utah's nearly 2.25 million residents.

ANSEL ADAMS TO CEDRIC WRIGHT

JUNE 10, 1937

The photographer Ansel Adams was renowned for his arrestingly clear black-and-white images of nature. On a return trip to his beloved Yosemite National Park, Adams was inspired to write to a friend, Cedric Wright.

Dear Cedric,

A strange thing happened to me today. I saw a big thundercloud move down over Half Dome, and it was so big and clear and brilliant that it made me see many things that were drifting around inside of me; things that related to those who are loved and those who are real friends.

For the first time I *know* what love is; what friends are; and what art should be.

Love is a seeking for a way of life; the way that cannot be followed alone; the resonance of all spiritual and physical things. Children are not only of flesh and blood—children may be ideas, thoughts, emotions. The person of the one who is loved is a form

composed of a myriad mirrors reflecting and illuminating the powers and the thoughts and the emotions that are within you, and flashing another kind of light from within. No words or deeds may encompass it.

Friendship is another form of love—more passive perhaps, but 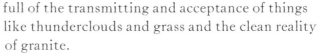 full of the transmitting and acceptance of things like thunderclouds and grass and the clean reality of granite.

Art is both love and friendship, and understanding; the desire to give. It is not charity, which is the giving of Things, it is more than kindness which is the giving of self. It is both the taking and giving of beauty, the turning out to the light the inner folds of the awareness of the spirit. It is the recreation on another plane of the realities of the world; the tragic and wonderful realities of earth and men, and of all the inter-relations of these.

I wish the thundercloud had moved up over Tahoe and let loose on you; I could wish you nothing finer.

Ansel

THE GRAPES OF WRATH

JOHN STEINBECK, 1939

THE CARS OF THE MIGRANT PEOPLE crawled out of the side roads onto the great cross-country highway, and they took the migrant way to the West. In the daylight they scuttled like bugs to the westward; and as the dark caught them, they clustered like bugs near to shelter and to water. And because they were lonely and perplexed, because they had all come from a place of sadness and worry and defeat, and because they were all going to a new mysterious place, they huddled together; they talked together; they shared their lives, their food, and the things they hoped for in the new country. Thus it might be that one family camped near a spring, and another camped for the spring and for company, and a third because two families had pioneered the place and found it good. And when the sun went down, perhaps twenty families and twenty cars were there.

In the evening a strange thing happened: the twenty families became one family, the children were the children of all. The loss of

THE GRAPES OF WRATH

home became one loss, and the golden time in the West was one dream. And it might be that a sick child threw despair into the hearts of twenty families, of a hundred people; that a birth there in a tent kept a hundred people quiet and awestruck through the night and filled a hundred people with the birth-joy in the morning. A family which the night before had been lost and fearful might search its goods to find a present for a new baby. In the evening, sitting about the fires, the twenty were one. They grew to be units of the camps, units of the evenings and the nights. A guitar unwrapped from a blanket and turned—and the songs, which were all of the people, were sung in the nights. Men sang the words, and women hummed the tunes.

Every night a world created, complete with furniture—friends made and enemies established; a world complete with braggarts and with cowards, with quiet men, with humble men, with kindly men. Every night relationships that make a world, established; and every morning the world torn down like a circus.

THE GRAPES OF WRATH

At first the families were timid in the building and tumbling worlds, but gradually the technique of building worlds became their technique. Then leaders emerged, then laws were made, then codes came into being. And as the worlds moved westward they were more complete and better furnished, for their builders were more experienced in building them.

The families learned what rights must be observed—the right of privacy in the tent; the right to keep the past black hidden in the heart; the right to talk and to listen; the right to refuse help or to accept, to offer help or to decline it; the right of son to court and daughter to be courted; the right of the hungry to be fed; the rights of the pregnant and the sick to transcend all other rights.

And the families learned, although no one told them, what rights are monstrous and must be destroyed: the right to intrude upon privacy, the right to be noisy while the camp slept, the right of seduction or rape, the right of adultery and theft and murder. These rights were crushed, because the little worlds could not exist for even a night with such rights alive.

And as the worlds moved westward, rules became laws,

although no one told the families. It is unlawful to foul near the camp; it is unlawful in any way to foul the drinking water; it is unlawful to eat good rich food near one who is hungry, unless he is asked to share.

And with the laws, the punishments—and there were only two—a quick and murderous fight or ostracism; and ostracism was the worst. For if one broke the laws his name and face went with him, and he had no place in any world, no matter where created.

In the worlds, social conduct became fixed and rigid, so that a man must say "Good morning" when asked for it, so that a man might have a willing girl if he stayed with her, if he fathered her children and protected them. But a man might not have one girl one night and another the next, for this would endanger the worlds.

The families moved westward, and the technique of building the worlds improved so that the people could be safe in their worlds; and the form was so fixed that a family acting in the rules knew it was safe in the rules.

There grew up government in the worlds, with leaders, with elders. A man who was wise found that his wisdom was needed in

THE GRAPES OF WRATH

every camp; a man who was a fool could not change his folly with his world. And a kind of insurance developed in these nights. A man with food fed a hungry man, and thus insured himself against hunger. And when a baby died a pile of silver coins grew at the door flap, for a baby must be well buried, since it has had nothing else of life. An old man may be left in a potter's field, but not a baby.

A certain physical pattern is needed for the building of a world—water, a river bank, a stream, a spring, or even a faucet unguarded. And there is needed enough flat land to pitch the tents, a little brush or wood to build the fires. If there is a garbage dump not too far off, all the better; for there can be found equipment—stove tops, a curved fender to shelter the fire, and cans to cook in and to eat from.

And the worlds were built in the evening. The people, moving in from the highways, made them with their tents and their hearts and their brains.

SOUTHERN FRIED CHICKEN
WITH CREAM GRAVY

The first recipe for this dish was published in *Virginia House-Wife* in 1828. When I was a child there was a magnificent Southern cook who once made Southern fried chicken with paprika in my mother's kitchen. I have spent years trying to recreate that chicken. Crisco was definitely one of the magic ingredients. Goes great with our mashed potatoes.

1 chicken, 3–4 pounds, cut into pieces

2 cups buttermilk

1 ½ cups all-purpose flour

2 tablespoons sea salt or 1 ½ teaspoons salt

¾ teaspoon pepper

2 tablespoons paprika

2 cups Crisco oil

½ cup bacon fat

2 cups milk

1. Coat the chicken with buttermilk in a bowl; cover and chill 6–8 hours.

2. Drain the chicken pieces, discarding the buttermilk.

3. Put ¾ cup flour, 1 teaspoon salt, ½ teaspoon pepper, and 2 tablespoons paprika in a big resealable plastic bag.

4. Heat the oil and bacon fat in a cast-iron or other heavy pot to 360° F (a medium boil). I like the sides of the pot to be high to reduce spatter.

5. Put the chicken pieces into the bag, a couple at a time, and shake until completely covered. Working in batches (the pieces shouldn't be

touching in the skillet) and using tongs, fry the chicken slowly until cooked through and a deep golden brown. Cook several minutes on each side, then turn them occasionally until they have cooked for 25–30 minutes. Keep them warm in the oven while you finish.

6. Drain the chicken pieces on paper towels, leaving $^{1}/_{4}$ cup of the drippings in the skillet.

7. Add $^{1}/_{4}$ cup flour to the drippings and cook, whisking constantly, over medium heat, until the gravy is golden brown.

8. Add milk gradually; cook, whisking constantly, for 3–5 minutes or until thickened and bubbly. Stir in the remaining $^{1}/_{2}$ teaspoon salt and remaining $^{1}/_{4}$ teaspoon pepper, and serve immediately.

Serves 4.

World War II

General George S. Patton (1885–1945) was nicknamed "Old Blood and Guts." Commanding the U.S. Third Army in Europe, he won a pivotal battle when he and his men drove the Germans back from France after the D-Day landings.

The U.S. was officially neutral until December 7, 1941, when the Japanese attacked Pearl Harbor. At dawn on Sunday, 360 planes attacked in two waves, sinking 16 ships and killing 2,400 military and civilian Americans.

On December 8, 1941, the U.S. declared war on Japan; similar declarations were made against Germany and Italy three days later.

Norman Rockwell's *Saturday Evening Post* cover depicting "Rosie the Riveter" (May 29, 1943) epitomized the spirit of the nearly 3 million women who entered war work, replacing men called into the armed forces.

On August 6, 1945, the American bomber *Enola Gay* dropped the first atomic bomb on Hiroshima, Japan, destroying 4.4 square miles. Three days later a second atomic bomb landed on Nagasaki. The two attacks killed and wounded more than 200,000. Japan sued for peace the next day.

Champion chess player Reuben Fine helped the war effort by calculating, on the basis of positional probability, where enemy submarines might surface.

More than 500 native Navajo "talkers" were enlisted by the Marines to serve in the Pacific. Navajo, impossible for the Japanese translate, also saved time because it needed minimal coding.

On April 29, 1945, American troops liberated 27,400 prisoners from the Dachau concentration camp. It's estimated another 50,000 died there.

During wartime sugar rationing, most soda companies scaled back production. Not so 7-UP which, being less sweet, required less sugar. Instead, it cashed in with a national advertising campaign.

It took two surrenders to end WWII. In Europe, Germany surrendered to General Eisenhower on May 7, 1945. But in the Pacific, the Japanese continued fighting until the atomic bomb was dropped, finally surrendering on August 14, 1945.

Of all the Americans who served in the armed forces, 6.6% were killed (407,316) or wounded (670,846).

"A Date Which Will Live in Infamy"

Franklin Delano Roosevelt, December 8, 1941

*The day after the attack on Pearl Harbor, President Roosevelt
asked the U.S. Congress to declare war against Japan.*

YESTERDAY, December 7, 1941—a date which will live in
infamy—the United States of America was suddenly and
deliberately attacked by naval and air forces of the Empire of Japan.

The United States was at peace with that nation and, at the
solicitation of Japan, was still in conversation with its Government
and its Emperor looking toward the maintenance of peace in the
Pacific. Indeed, one hour after Japanese air squadrons had
commenced bombing in Oahu, the Japanese Ambassador to the
United States and his colleague delivered to the Secretary of State
a formal reply to a recent American message. While this reply
stated that it seemed useless to continue the existing diplomatic
negotiations, it contained no threat or hint of war or armed attack.

It will be recorded that the distance of Hawaii from Japan makes it obvious that the attack was deliberately planned many days or even weeks ago. During the intervening time the Japanese government has deliberately sought to deceive the United States by false statements and expressions of hope for continued peace.

The attack yesterday on the Hawaiian islands has caused severe damage to American naval and military forces. Very many American lives have been lost. In addition American ships have been reported torpedoed on the high seas between San Francisco and Honolulu.

Yesterday the Japanese government also launched an attack against Malaya. Last night Japanese forces attacked Hong Kong. Last night Japanese forces attacked Guam. Last night Japanese forces attacked the Philippine Islands. Last night the Japanese attacked Wake Island. This morning the Japanese attacked Midway Island.

Japan has, therefore, undertaken a surprise offensive extending throughout the Pacific area. The facts of yesterday speak for themselves. The people of the United States have already formed their opinions and well understand the implications to the very life and safety of our nation.

As Commander-In-Chief of the Army and Navy, I have directed that all measures be taken for our defense.

Always will we remember the character of the onslaught against us.

No matter how long it may take us to overcome this premeditated invasion, the American people in their righteous might will win through to absolute victory.

I believe I interpret the will of the Congress and of the people when I assert that we will not only defend ourselves to the uttermost but will make very certain that this form of treachery shall never endanger us again.

Hostilities exist. There is no blinking at the fact that our people, our territory and our interests are in grave danger.

With confidence in our armed forces—with the unbonded determination of our people—we will gain the inevitable triumph—so help us God.

I ask that the Congress declare that since the unprovoked and dastardly attack by Japan on Sunday, December seventh, a state of war has existed between the United States and the Japanese Empire.

Two Soldiers

WILLIAM FAULKNER, 1942

W E WAS STILL SOWING the vetch then that ought to been all finished by the fifteenth of November, because pap was still behind, just like he had been ever since me and Pete had knowed him. And we had firewood to git in, too, but every night me and Pete would go down to Old Man Killegrew's and stand outside his parlor window in the cold and listen to his radio; then we would come back home and lay in the bed and Pete would tell me what it was. That is, he would tell me for a while. Then he wouldn't tell me. It was like he didn't want to talk about it no more. He would tell me to shut up because he wanted to go to sleep, but he never wanted to go to sleep.

He would lay there, a heap stiller than if he was asleep, and it would be something, I could feel it coming out of him, like he was mad at me even, only I knowed he wasn't thinking about me, or like he was worried about something, and it wasn't that neither, because he never had nothing to worry about. He never got behind like pap,

TWO SOLDIERS

let alone stayed behind. Pap give him ten acres when he graduated from the Consolidated, and me and Pete both reckoned pap was durn glad to get shut of at least ten acres, less to have to worry with himself; and Pete had them ten acres all sowed to vetch and busted out and bedded for the winter, and so it wasn't that. But it was something. And still we would go down to Old Man Killegrew's every night and listen to his radio, and they was at it in the Philippines now, but General MacArthur was holding um. Then we would come back home and lay in the bed, and Pete wouldn't tell me nothing or talk at all. He would just lay there still as a ambush and when I would touch him, his side or his leg would feel hard and still as iron, until after a while I would go to sleep.

Then one night—it was the first time he had said nothing to me except to jump on me about not chopping enough wood at the wood tree where we was cutting—he said, "I got to go."

"Go where?" I said.

"To that war," Pete said.

"Before we even finish gettin' in the firewood?"

"Firewood, hell," Pete said.

Two Soldiers

"All right," I said. "When we going to start?"

But he wasn't even listening. He laid there, hard and still as iron in the dark. "I got to go," he said. "I just ain't going to put up with no folks treating the Unity States that way."

"Yes," I said. "Firewood or no firewood, I reckon we got to go."

This time he heard me. He laid still again, but it was a different kind of still.

"You?" he said. "To a war?"

"You'll whup the big uns and I'll whup the little uns," I said.

Then he told me I couldn't go. At first I thought he just never wanted me tagging after him, like he wouldn't leave me go with him when he went sparking them girls of Tull's. Then he told me the Army wouldn't leave me go because I was too little, and then I knowed he really meant it and that I couldn't go nohow noways. And somehow I hadn't believed until then that he was going himself, but now I knowed he was and that he wasn't going to leave me go with him a-tall.

"I'll chop the wood and tote the water for you-all then!" I said. "You got to have wood and water!"

Two Soldiers

Anyway, he was listening to me now. He wasn't like iron now.

He turned onto his side and put his hand on my chest because it was me that was laying straight and hard on my back now.

"No," he said. "You got to stay here and help pap."

"Help him what?" I said. "He ain't never caught up nohow. He can't get no further behind. He can sholy take care of this little shirttail of a farm while me and you are whupping them Japanese. I got to go too. If you got to go, then so have I."

"No," Pete said. "Hush now. Hush." And he meant it, and I knowed he did. Only I made sho from his own mouth. I quit.

"So I just can't go then," I said.

"No," Pete said. "You just can't go. You're too little, in the first place, and in the second place—"

"All right," I said. "Then shut up and leave me go to sleep."

So he hushed then and laid back. And I laid there like I was already asleep, and pretty soon he was asleep and I knowed it was the wanting to go to the war that had worried him and kept him awake, and now that he had decided to go, he wasn't worried any more.

Iwao Matsushita to Attorney General Francis Biddle

Fort Missoula, Montana, January 2, 1943

During World War II, the U.S. government forced 120,000 Japanese Americans to leave their homes and live in internment camps. Iwao Matsushita, one such victim, was detained in Montana; his wife was detained in Idaho. A year after the letter excerpted here was written, they were reunited. Not until 1988 did Washington issue a formal apology.

Dear Mr. Biddle,

I, Iwao Matsushita, an alien Japanese, have been detained in Fort Missoula, since Dec. 28, 1941, and I was recently notified about my internment order, despite the fact the Hearing Board made a recommendation for my release.

Since I read your article in a magazine last spring, regarding your policy of treating "alien enemies"—the words, you mentioned, you even didn't like to use— you have been occupying the innermost shrine of my heart as my only refuge and savior. So when I received your internment order, I was naturally greatly disappointed, because according to your interpretation in the magazine, you intern only those aliens whom you consider to be potentially dangerous to the public safety.

Now, my conscience urges me to make a personal heart-to-heart appeal to you. Kindly allow me to make a brief statement about myself.

I was born a Christian in a Methodist minister's family, educated in an American Mission School, came to this country in 1919 from sheer admiration of the American way of life. I have always been living, almost half and best part of my life, in Seattle, Wash., and never went to Japan for the last twenty-four years, despite the fact there were many such opportunities, simply because I liked this country, and the principles on which it stands.

I have never broken any Federal, State, Municipal, or even traffic laws, and paid taxes regularly. I believe myself one of the most upright persons. I have never been, am not, and will never be potentially dangerous to the safety of the United States. . . .

On the contrary I have done much good to the American public. For instance, several years ago, I taught Japanese Language in the University of Washington, Seattle, without any compensation to help out the institution, which couldn't get appropriation for that purpose from the State. . . .

My wife, with whom I have never been separated even for a short time during the last twenty-five years, and who has the same loyalty and admiration for this country, is living helplessly and sorrowfully in Idaho Relocation Center. You are the only person who can make us join in happiness and let us continue to enjoy the American life.

Therefore, please give my case your special reconsideration and let me anticipate your favorable answer.

Yours respectfully,
Iwao Matsushita

DEMOCRACY

E.B. WHITE. JULY 3, 1944

Written as an editorial in The New Yorker.

WE RECEIVED A LETTER from the Writers' War Board the other day asking for a statement on "The Meaning of Democracy." It presumably is our duty to comply with such a request, and it is certainly our pleasure.

Surely the Board knows what democracy is. It is the line that forms on the right. It is the don't in Don't Shove. It is the hole in the stuffed shirt through which the sawdust slowly trickles; it is the dent in the high hat. Democracy is the recurrent suspicion that more than half of the people are right more than half of the time. It is the feeling of privacy in the voting booths, the feeling of communion in the libraries, the feeling of vitality everywhere. Democracy is the score at the beginning of the ninth. It is an idea which hasn't been disproved yet, a song the words of which have not gone bad. It's the mustard on the hot dog and the cream in the rationed coffee. Democracy is a request from a War Board, in the middle of a morning in the middle of a war, wanting to know what democracy is.

DON'T FENCE ME IN

COLE PORTER, 1944

Wild Cat Kelly, looking mighty pale,
Was standing by the sherriff's side,
And when the sherriff said, "I'm sending you to jail,
Wild Cat raised his head and cried:

Chorus
Oh, give me land, lots of land under starry skies above,
Don't fence me in.
Let me ride thru the wide-open country that I love,
Don't fence me in.
Let me be by myself in the evening breeze,
Listen to the murmur of the cottonwood trees,
Send me off forever, but I ask you, please,
Don't fence me in.

Just turn me loose,
Let me straddle my old saddle underneath the Western skies.
On my cayuse,
Let me wander over yonder till I see the mountains rise.
I want to ride to the ridge where the West commences,
Gaze at the moon till I lose my senses,
Can't look at hobbles and I can't stand fences,
Don't fence me in.

Wild Cat Kelly, back again in town,
Was sitting by his sweetheart's side,
And when his sweetheart said, "Come on, let's settle down,"
Wildcat raised his head and cried:

(Chorus)

"George," an African American Soldier, to His Sister

France, March 19, 1945

More than a million African Americans fought in World War II, although they had to do it in segregated units. In a letter excerpted here, one such soldier wrote that despite the treatment he had received, he was proud to be serving his country.

Dear Sis:

*D*on't be surprised when you receive this letter and find that I am giving serious thought to our race, its problems and its contributions to the welfare of mankind. I shall hope to be able to write a series of letters of this nature....

All of us have many reasons for wanting to stay in the States. Yet we know that the war can't be won by our attending dances and enjoying weekend passes. Yes, we too are "Red

Blooded Americans" and have as much at stake as anybody. Yes, we have a share in the American Way of Life. We came from all parts of America but we are still Americans. We hope that the American People won't forget that if we can work and fight for the Democratic Way, that we are entitled to enjoy every privilege it affords when this mess is over. . . .

Victory is in sight. We are all confident in the ability of our men "Up Front." I thank God for giving the soldier of color the intestinal fortitude to go on and do a good job in spite of the odds that have been against him. We still have men fighting and dying in the Theatres of War. The colored men stuck to their assigned jobs; if they didn't the men "Up Front" would have known better than anyone else. In closing, Sis, I will write a few words penned by the great Negro poet Dunbar, "Out of the hell and dawn of it all, cometh good."

Best wishes,
Your Brother
George

Platitudes

"That's one small step for man;
one giant leap for mankind."
—*Neil Armstrong*

"No one can make you feel
inferior without your consent."
—*Eleanor Roosevelt*

"Speak softly and carry a big stick;
you will go far."
—*Theodore Roosevelt*

"We have too many high-sounding
words, and too few actions that
correspond with them."
—*Abigail Adams*

"Tragedy is if I cut my finger,
comedy is if you walk into
an open sewer and die."
—*Mel Brooks*

"As long as the world shall last there
will be wrongs, and if no man
objected and no man rebelled, those
wrongs would last forever."
—*Clarence Darrow*

"Genius is 1% inspiration
and 99% perspiration."
—*Thomas Edison*

"We are just an advanced breed of
monkeys on a minor planet of a
very average star. But we can understand the Universe. That makes us
something very special."
—*Stephen Hawking*

"The world is a fine place
and worth the fighting for
and I hate very much to leave it."
—*Ernest Hemingway*

"Where liberty dwells,
there is my country."
—*Benjamin Franklin*

"God grants liberty only to
those who love it, and are always
ready to guard and defend it."
—*Daniel Webster*

"The limits of tyrants are
prescribed by the endurance
of those whom they oppress."
—*Frederick Douglass*

"Information is the
currency of democracy."
—*Thomas Jefferson*

"Time flies like an arrow;
fruit flies like a banana."
—*Groucho Marx*

"War is hell."
—*William Tecumseh Sherman*

"If you once forfeit the
confidence of your fellow
citizens, you can never regain
their respect and esteem.
You may fool all of the people
some of the time; you can even
fool some of the people all
the time; but you can't fool all
of the people all of the time."
—*Abraham Lincoln*

"The business of America
is business."
—*Calvin Coolidge*

"Whenever you find you
are on the side of the majority,
it is time to pause
and reflect."
—*Mark Twain*

"The first duty of a revolutionary
is to get away with it."
—*Abbie Hoffman*

BARBECUED RIBS

American barbecue was first popularized on the cattle drives of the late 1800s, when cowboys slow-roasted tough meat to make it more palatable. The barbecue sauce was created using a New World staple: tomatoes.

3 cups ketchup

1 cup chili sauce

grated zest of 1 lemon

Juice of 2 large lemon

1/4 cup French's mustard

1 1/2 tablespoons Tabasco sauce

1/4 cup Worcestershire sauce

2 tablespoons molasses

2 tablespoons brown sugar

2 cloves garlic, chopped

1/4 cup chopped parsley

2 tablespoons apple cider vinegar

salt and pepper to taste

3 pounds beef ribs

1. In a large heavy skillet, combine all of the ingredients (except the ribs) and warm through over low heat. Do not bring to a boil.

2. Remove, cool and use half the mixture to rub all sides of the meat 1 hour before grilling.

3. Prepare the grill and ignite the charcoal.

4. Grill the ribs over medium–hot coals until tender (1 hour or so). Keep basting and make sure you turn them frequently so they don't burn.

5. Continue cooking for 20–25 minutes until done. (You can also do these in the oven: preheat oven to 325° F and place the ribs in a shallow baking pan. Cover with half the sauce. Bake in the center of the oven for 1–1 1/2 hour depending on the size. Turn and baste frequently with the remaining sauce.)

Serves 6 to 8.

Potato Salad

¹/₃ cup chicken stock

2 tablespoons cider vinegar

2 pounds large potatoes, peeled, cooked and sliced

1 cup mayonnaise

2 tablespoons Dijon mustard

²/₃ cup finely chopped scallions

¹/₂ cup finely chopped celery

3 tablespoons or so finely chopped fresh chives

salt and pepper to taste

1. Mix the chicken stock and the vinegar and pour over the potatoes.

2. In a separate bowl, mix the mayonnaise and Dijon mustard. Add the scallions, celery and chives. Combine with the potatoes, mixing gently.

3. Season to taste with salt and pepper.

4. Cover and refrigerate for at least an hour. Let stand at room temperature for 20 minutes before serving.

5. Serve with barbecued ribs and slices of fresh watermelon.

Serves 4 to 6.

"If by Whiskey"

Noah S. Sweat, Mississippi, 1948

Although Prohibition had been repealed, it was still a big political issue in Mississippi in 1948, when Noah Sweat was campaigning for the office of state representative in Alcorn County. So Sweat gave a speech intended to appeal to both sides of the issue. He won the election, and went on serve as prosecutor and eventually Judge of the First Judicial District.

MY FRIENDS, I had not intended to discuss this controversial subject at this particular time. However, I want you to know that I do not shun controversy. On the contrary, I will take a stand on any issue at any time, regardless of how fraught with controversy it might be. You have asked me how I feel about whisky. All right, here is how I feel about whisky.

If when you say "whisky" you mean the devil's brew, the poison scourge, the bloody monster that defiles innocence, dethrones reason, destroys the home, creates misery and poverty, yea, literally takes the bread from the mouths of little children; if you mean the evil drink that topples the Christian man and woman from the pinnacle of righteous, gracious living into the bottomless pit of degradation, and despair, and shame, and helplessness, and hopelessness—then certainly I am against it.

But, if when you say "whisky" you mean the oil of conversation, the philosophic wine, the ale that is consumed when good fellows get together, that puts a song in their hearts and laughter on their lips, and the warm glow of contentment in their eyes; if you mean Christmas cheer; if you mean the stimulating drink that puts the spring into the old gentleman's step on a frosty, crispy morning; if you mean the drink that enables a man to magnify his joy, and his happiness, and to forget, if only for a little while, life's great tragedies, and heartaches, and sorrows; if you mean that drink the sale of which pours into our treasuries untold millions of dollars, which are used to provide tender care for our little crippled children, our blind, our deaf, our dumb, our pitiful aged and infirm; to build highways and hospitals and schools—then certainly I am for it.

This is my stand. I will not retreat from it. I will not compromise.

Line Up For Yesterday: An ABC of Baseball Immortals

Ogden Nash, 1949

A is for Alex
The great Alexander;
More goose eggs he pitched
Than a popular gander.

B is for Bresnahan
Back of the plate;
The Cubs were his love,
And McGraw was his hate.

C is for Cobb,
Who grew spikes and not corn,
And made all the basemen
Wish they weren't born.

D is for Dean.
The grammatical Diz,
When they asked, Who's the tops?
Said correctly, I is.

E is for Evers,
His jaw in advance;
Never afraid
To Tinker with Chance.

F is for Fordham
And Frankie and Frisch
I wish he were back
With the Giants, I wish.

G is for Gehrig,
The Pride of the Stadium;
His record pure gold,
His courage, pure radium.

H is for Hornsby;
When pitching to Rog,
The pitcher would pitch,
Then the pitcher would dodge.

I is for Me,
Not a hard-sitting man,
But an outstanding all-time
Incurable fan.

J is for Johnson
The Big Train in his prime
Was so fast he could throw
Three strikes at a time.

K is for Keeler,
As fresh as green paint,
The fustest and mostest
To hit where they ain't.

L is Lajoie
Whom Clevelanders love,
Napoleon himself,
With glue in his glove.

M IS FOR MATTY,
WHO CARRIED A CHARM
IN THE FORM OF AN EXTRA
BRAIN IN HIS ARM.

N IS FOR NEWSOM,
BOBO'S FAVORITE KIN.
IF YOU ASK HOW HE'S HERE,
HE TALKED HIMSELF IN.

O IS FOR OTT
OF THE RESTLESS RIGHT FOOT.
WHEN HE LEANED ON THE PELLET,
THE PELLET STAYED PUT.

P IS FOR PLANK,
THE ARM OF THE A'S;
WHEN HE TANGLED WITH MATTY
GAMES LASTED FOR DAYS.

Q IS DON QUIXOTE
CORNELIUS MACK;
NEITHER YANKEES NOR YEARS
CAN HALT HIS ATTACK.

R IS FOR RUTH.
TO TELL YOU THE TRUTH,
THERE'S NO MORE TO BE SAID,
JUST R IS FOR RUTH.

S IS FOR SPEAKER,
SWIFT CENTER-FIELD TENDER;
WHEN THE BALL SAW HIM COMING,
IT YELLED, "I SURRENDER."

T IS FOR TERRY
THE GIANT FROM MEMPHIS
WHOSE 400 AVERAGE
YOU CAN'T OVEREMPHIS.

U WOULD BE UBBELL
IF CARL WERE A COCKNEY;
WE SAY HUBBELL AND BASEBALL
LIKE FOOTBALL AND ROCKNE.

V IS FOR VANCE
THE DODGERS' OWN DAZZY;
NONE OF HIS RIVALS
COULD THROW AS FAST AS HE.

W, WAGNER,
THE BOWLEGGED BEAUTY;
SHORT WAS CLOSED TO ALL TRAFFIC
WITH HONUS ON DUTY.

X IS THE FIRST
OF TWO X'S IN FOXX
WHO WAS RIGHT BEHIND RUTH
WITH HIS POWERFUL SOXX.

Y IS FOR YOUNG
THE MAGNIFICENT CY;
PEOPLE BATTED AGAINST HIM,
BUT I NEVER KNEW WHY.

Z IS FOR ZENITH,
THE SUMMIT OF FAME.
THESE MEN ARE UP THERE,
THESE MEN ARE THE GAME.

Villains

Benedict Arnold (1741–1801) led important battles in the revolution. But in 1780 it was revealed that he'd once offered to surrender a fort to the British. Thus labeled a traitor, he escaped to England.

John Wilkes Booth (1838–1865), actor and staunch Confederate, shot and killed President Lincoln at Ford's Theater. Booth was caught and shot soon after.

Both a relentless outlaw and a family man to the end, Jesse James (1847–1882) was a stagecoach- and bank-robbing cowboy and, some say, the "Robin Hood of the Wild West."

Robert LeRoy Parker, *aka* Butch Cassidy (1866–1908), and Harry Longabaugh, *aka* the Sundance Kid (1867–1908), led a band of gunslinging, train- and bank-robbing outlaws called the Wild Bunch. Legend has it that they met their end in a shootout in Bolivia.

Al "Scarface" Capone (1899-1947), dominated organized crime in Chicago in the late 1920s. After seven years in jail for tax evasion, he was weakened by syphilis and never returned to the underworld.

Bugsy Siegel (1906–1947) and Meyer Lansky (1902–1983) ruled the crime roost of Depression-era New York, and were early investors in Las Vegas. Lansky had Bugsy offed over his "creative bookkeeping" at the Flamingo Hotel and Casino, then went on to enjoy a long life of crime.

Senator Joseph McCarthy (1908–1957) ruined careers in Washington and Hollywood by accusing hundreds of communist affiliations. He was ultimately censured by the Senate.

Bonnie Parker (1910–1934), Clyde Barrow (1909–1934) and their gang blew through five states robbing banks and stores and gunning down whoever got in their way. They were ambushed and killed in Louisiana.

In 1972, President Richard "Tricky Dick" Nixon (1913–1994) gave the order that would end his presidency. The break-in of the Democratic Campaign Headquarters in the Watergate complex led to his resignation in 1974.

*

Lee Harvey Oswald (1939–1963) was arrested for shooting JFK from the window of the Dallas Book Depository on November 22, 1963. Three days later Oswald was killed by Jack Ruby at the Dallas County Jail.

*

On April 4, 1968, escaped convict James Earl Ray (1928–1998) assassinated Martin Luther King, Jr. Though Ray confessed, he later recanted and was never tried. He died in prison 30 years later.

Charles Manson (1934–), led Manson Family cult members on a 1969 murder spree in Hollywood that included Roman Polanski's pregnant wife, the actress Sharon Tate, and her guests.

Serial killer Jeffrey Dahmer (1960–1994) was arrested in 1991 after police found evidence of dismemberment, cannibalism, necrophilia and the parts of 17 victims in his apartment. Dahmer was murdered in prison.

DIVE FOR DREAMS

E.E. CUMMINGS, 1952

DIVE FOR DREAMS
OR A SLOGAN MAY TOPPLE YOU
(TREES ARE THEIR ROOTS
AND WIND IS WIND)

TRUST YOUR HEART
IF THE SEAS CATCH FIRE
(AND LIVE BY LOVE
THOUGH THE STARS WALK BACKWARD)

HONOUR THE PAST
BUT WELCOME THE FUTURE
(AND DANCE YOUR DEATH
AWAY AT THIS WEDDING)

NEVER MIND A WORLD
WITH ITS VILLAINS OR HEROES
(FOR GOD LIKES GIRLS
AND TOMORROW AND THE EARTH)

FROM

BREAKFAST AT TIFFANY'S

TRUMAN CAPOTE, 1956

T HAT MONDAY IN OCTOBER, 1943. A beautiful day with the buoyancy of a bird. To start, we had Manhattans at Joe Bells; and, when he heard of my good luck, champagne cocktails on the house. Later, we wandered toward Fifth Avenue, where there was a parade. The flags in the wind, the thump of military bands and military feet, seemed to have nothing to do with war, but to be, rather, a fanfare arranged in my personal honor.

We ate lunch at the cafeteria in the park. Afterwards, avoiding the zoo (Holly said she couldn't bear to see anything in a cage), we giggled, ran, sang along the paths toward the old wooden boathouse, now gone. Leaves floated on the lake; on the shore, a park-man was fanning a bonfire of them, and the smoke, rising like Indian signals, was the only smudge on the quivering air. Aprils have never meant much to me, autumns seem that season of beginning, spring; which is how I felt sitting with Holly on the railings of the boathouse porch. I thought of the future, and spoke of the past. Because Holly wanted to know about my childhood. She talked of her own, too; but it was elusive, nameless, placeless, an impressionistic recital, though the impression received was contrary to what one expected, for she gave an almost voluptuous account of swimming and summer, Christmas trees, pretty cousins and parties: in short, happy in a way that she was not, and never, certainly, the background of a child who had run away.

Or, I asked, wasn't it true that she'd been out on her own since she was fourteen? She rubbed her nose. "That's true. The other isn't. But really, darling, you made such a tragedy out of *your* childhood I didn't feel I should compete."

She hopped off the railing. "Anyway, it reminds me: I ought to send Fred some peanut butter." The rest of the afternoon we were east and west worming out of reluctant grocers cans of peanut butter, a wartime scarcity; dark came before we'd rounded up a

Breakfast at Tiffany's

half-dozen jars, the last at a delicatessen on Third Avenue.
It was near the antique shop with the palace of a bird cage in its
window, so I took her there to see it, and she enjoyed the point,
its fantasy: "But still, it's a cage."

Passing a Woolworth's, she gripped my arm: "Let's steal
something," she said, pulling me into the store, where at once
there seemed a pressure of eyes, as though we were already
under suspicion. "Come on. Don't be chicken." She scouted a
counter piled with paper pumpkins and Halloween masks. The
saleslady was occupied with a group of nuns who were trying on
masks. Holly picked up a mask and slipped it over her face; she
chose another and put it on mine; then she took my hand and
we walked away. It was as simple as that. Outside, we ran a few
blocks, I think to make it more dramatic; but also because, as
I'd discovered, successful theft exhilarates. I wondered if she'd
often stolen. "I used to," she said. "I mean I had to. If I wanted
anything. But I still do it every now and then, sort of to keep
my hand in."

We wore the masks all the way home.

Vietnam

American determination to stem the spread of communism in Asia led to direct involvement in Vietnam when the first American "advisors" arrived in 1955.

✳

The U.S. Air Force first deployed the defoliant Agent Orange (named for its orange metal containers) in 1962, in an effort to expose Vietcong trails and roads.

✳

Covert U.S. and South Vietnamese naval operations began in early 1965. "Operation Rolling Thunder"—sustained bombing raids of North Vietnam—began in February and continued for three years.

✳

The first Marines arrived in Danang, Vietnam in 1965.

✳

Protests weren't just for radicals and hippies: as early as 1966, veterans of World Wars I and II and the Korean War rallied in New York against American involvement in Vietnam.

✳

Recruiters from Dow Chemical, the manufacturer of Napalm, were driven from the University of Wisconsin at Madison in 1967, amid massive student protests.

✳

On January 31, 1968, the North Vietnamese launched the surprise Tet Offensive. Though U.S. forces ultimately pushed back the communists, the event revealed how badly America had underestimated the Vietcong.

Charlie Company, 11th Brigade, American Division, slaughtered more than 300 civilians in the village of My Lai on March 16, 1968. A shocked America only learned of the infamous massacre a year later. Commanding officer Lt. William Calley was convicted of murder in 1971.

"Operation Breakfast" was a covert bombing campaign in Cambodia ordered by President Nixon in 1969, without the knowledge of Congress or the American people.

On May 4, 1970, four students were killed and eight others wounded when National Guardsmen opened fire on an antiwar demonstration at Ohio's Kent State University.

The New York Times published the Pentagon Papers in 1971. Leaked from inside the government, they detailed years of deception by the U.S. military and the White House concerning America's policy in Vietnam.

Nixon ordered the demobilization of 70,000 troops 1972. In 1973, Henry Kissinger and North Vietnam's Le Duc Tho signed a cease-fire agreement. Congressional hearings on the bombing of Cambodia resulted in an order to stop all such bombings on August 15, 1973.

The last American troops were evacuated from Saigon in 1975, as the city fell to communist forces.

For the U.S., the war produced more than 2 million veterans, took more than 58,000 lives and cost more than $150 billion.

THE JOY LUCK CLUB

AMY TAN, 1989 (SET IN THE 1960S)

I WAS SIX WHEN my mother taught me the art of invisible strength. It was strategy for winning arguments, respect from others, and eventually, though neither of us knew it at the time, chess games.

"Bite back your tongue," scolded my mother when I cried loudly, yanking her hand toward the store that sold bags of salted plums. At home, she said, "Wise guy, he not go against wind. In Chinese we say, Come from South, blow with wind—poom!— North will follow. Strongest wind cannot be seen."

The next week I bit back my tongue as we entered the store with the forbidden candies. When my mother finished her shop- ping, she quietly plucked a small bag of plums from the rack and put it on the counter with the rest of the items.

My mother imparted her daily truths so she could help my older brothers and me rise above our circumstances. We lived in San

Francisco's Chinatown. Like most of the other Chinese children who played in the back alleys of restaurants and curio shops, I didn't think we were poor. My bowl was always full, three five-course meals every day, beginning with a soup full of mysterious things I didn't want to know the names of.

We lived on Waverly Place, in a warm, clean, two-bedroom flat that sat above a small Chinese bakery specializing in steamed pastries and dim sum. In the early morning, when the alley was still quiet, I could smell fragrant red beans as they were cooked down to a pasty sweetness. By daybreak, our flat was heavy with the odor of fried sesame balls and sweet curried chicken crescents. From my bed, I would listen as my father got ready for work, then locked the door behind him, one-two-three clicks.

At the end of our two-block alley was a small sandlot playground with swings and slides well-shined down the middle with use. The play area was bordered by wood-slat benches where old-country people sat cracking roasted watermelon seeds with their golden teeth and scattering the husks to an impatient gathering of gurgling pigeons. The best playground, however, was the dark alley itself. It was crammed with daily mysteries and adventures. My brothers and I would peer into the medicinal herb shop, watching old Li dole out onto a stiff sheet of white paper the right amount of insect shells, saffron-colored seeds, and pungent leaves for his ailing customers. It was said that he once cured a woman dying of an ancestral curse that had eluded the best of American doctors. Next to the pharmacy was a printer who specialized in gold-embossed wedding invitations and festive red banners.

Farther down the street was Ping Yuen Fish Market. The front window displayed a tank crowded with doomed fish and turtles struggling to gain footing on the slimy green-tiled sides. A hand-written sign informed tourists, "Within this store, is all for food, not for pet." Inside, the butchers with their blood-stained white smocks deftly gutted the fish while customers cried out their orders and shouted, "Give me your freshest," to which the butchers always protested, "All are freshest." On less crowded market days, we would inspect the crates of live frogs and crabs which we were warned not to poke, boxes of dried cuttlefish, and row upon row of iced prawns, squid, and slippery fish. The sanddabs made me shiver each time; their eyes lay on one flattened side and reminded me of my mother's story of a careless girl who ran into a crowded street and was crushed by a cab. "Was smash flat," reported my mother.

At the corner of the alley was Hong Sing's, a four-table café with a recessed stairwell in front that led to a door marked "Tradesmen." My brothers and I believed the bad people emerged from this door at night. Tourists never went to Hong Sing's, since the menu was printed only in Chinese. A Caucasian man with a big camera once posed me and my playmates in front of the restaurant. He had us move to the side of the picture window so the photo would capture the roasted duck with its head dangling from a juice-covered rope. After he took the picture, I told him he should go into Hong Sing's and eat dinner. When he smiled and asked me what they served, I shouted, "Guts and duck's feet and octopus gizzards!" Then I ran off with my friends, shrieking with laughter as we scampered across the alley and hid in the entryway grotto of the China Gem Company, my heart pounding with hope that he would chase us.

My mother named me after the street that we lived on: Waverly Place Jong, my official name for important American documents.

But my family called me Meimei, "Little Sister." I was the youngest, the only daughter. Each morning before school, my mother would twist and yank on my thick black hair until she had formed two tightly wound pigtails. One day, as she struggled to weave a hard-toothed comb through my disobedient hair, I had a sly thought.

I asked her, "Ma, what is Chinese torture?" My mother shook her head. A bobby pin was wedged between her lips. She wetted her palm and smoothed the hair above my ear, then pushed the pin in so that it nicked sharply against my scalp.

"Who say this word?" she asked without a trace of knowing how wicked I was being. I shrugged my shoulders and said, "Some boy in my class said Chinese people do Chinese torture."

"Chinese people do many things," she said simply. "Chinese people do business, do medicine, do painting. Not lazy like American people. We do torture. Best torture."

"Ask Not What Your Country Can Do For You"

John F. Kennedy, Washington, D.C., January 20, 1961

At 43, John F. Kennedy was the youngest president elected in U.S. history. In his inaugural address, he called for a patriotic brand of action.

WE OBSERVE TODAY not a victory of party but a celebration of freedom—symbolizing an end as well as a beginning—signifying renewal as well as change. For I have sworn before you and Almighty God the same solemn oath our forebears prescribed nearly a century and three quarters ago.

The world is very different now. For man holds in his mortal hands the power to abolish all forms of human poverty and all forms of human life. And yet the same revolutionary beliefs for which our forebears fought are still at issue around the globe—the belief that the rights of man come not from the generosity of the state but from the hand of God.

We dare not forget today that we are the heirs of that first revolution. Let the word go forth from this time and place, to

friend and foe alike, that the torch has been passed to a new generation of Americans—born in this century, tempered by war, disciplined by a hard and bitter peace, proud of our ancient heritage—and unwilling to witness or permit the slow undoing of those human rights to which this Nation has always been committed, and to which we are committed today at home and around the world.

Let every nation know, whether it wishes us well or ill, that we shall pay any price, bear any burden, meet any hardship, support any friend, oppose any foe to assure the survival and the success of liberty....

In your hands, my fellow citizens, more than mine, will rest the final success or failure of our course. Since this country was founded, each generation of Americans has been summoned to give testimony to its national loyalty. The graves of young Americans who answered the call to service surround the globe.

Now the trumpet summons us again—not as a call to bear arms, though arms we need—not as a call to battle, though embattled we are—but a call to bear the burden of a long twilight struggle, year in and year out, "rejoicing in hope, patient in tribulation"—a struggle against the common enemies of man: tyranny, poverty, disease and war itself.

Can we forge against these enemies a grand and global alliance, North and South, East and West, that can assure a more fruitful life for all mankind? Will you join in that historic effort?

In the long history of the world, only a few generations have been granted the role of defending freedom in its hour of maximum danger. I do not shrink from this responsibility—I welcome it. I do not believe that any of us would exchange places with any other people or any other generation. The energy, the faith, the devotion which we bring to this endeavor will light our country and all who serve it—and the glow from that fire can truly light the world.

And so, my fellow Americans: Ask not what your country can do for you—ask what you can do for your country.

My fellow citizens of the world: Ask not what America will do for you, but what together we can do for the freedom of man.

Finally, whether you are citizens of America or citizens of the world, ask of us here the same high standards of strength and sacrifice which we ask of you. With a good conscience our only sure reward, with history the final judge of our deeds, let us go forth to lead the land we love, asking His blessing and His help, but knowing that here on earth God's work must truly be our own.

Washington, D.C.

☆

Irish-American architect James Hoban won a 1792 competition for the design of the White House. After the British attacked and burned the building down to a shell in 1812, Hoban oversaw the restoration.

☆

Telephones outnumber residents in the nation's capital.

☆

Ironically, Washington, D.C.— our nation's capital—has no voting representation in Congress.

☆

There aren't any skyscrapers in Washington D.C. because a city ordinance says the Washington Monument—at 555 feet high— must always be visible.

☆

Construction of the Washington Monument began in 1848 but wasn't completed until 34 years later. Protests over marble donated by Pope Pius IX and succeeding political squabbling stopped work for 26 years. The Monument finally opened to the public in 1888.

Sixty years to the day before terrorists flew a plane into the Pentagon (September 11, 2001), ground was broken in Arlington, Virginia for what was then called "The War Department."

Sprawling over more than 583 acres, the Pentagon is the world's largest office complex.

At George Washington's request, in 1791, the French civil engineer Pierre L'Enfant designed a plan for "Federal City," which would become Washington, D.C. A year later, Washington fired L'Enfant for insisting on complete control of the project.

D.C. became the permanent capital on December 1, 1800. Before that, the seat of government moved among seven different cities: New York, York, Lancaster, Baltimore, Annapolis, Princeton, Trenton and Philadelphia.

There are 132 rooms in the White House, of which 35 are bathrooms. Originally known as the "Executive Mansion," it was dubbed the White House in 1901 by Theodore Roosevelt.

The U.S. Capitol Building, which has no formal address, has 365 steps: one for each day of the year.

WILLIAM LEDERER TO ADMIRAL DAVID MCDONALD

1962

William Lederer is the co-author of The Ugly American *(1958), which portrayed the boorish side of Americans overseas. Four years after its publication, he had an experience while traveling in France with his family that prompted his writing to the Chief of U.S. Naval Operations.*

Admiral David L. McDonald, USN
Chief of Naval Operations
Washington, D.C.

Dear Admiral McDonald,

*E*ighteen people asked me to write this letter to you.

Last year at Christmas time, my wife, three boys and I were in France, on our way from Paris to Nice. For five wretched days everything had gone wrong. Our hotels were "tourist traps," our rented car broke down; we were all restless and irritable in the crowded car. On Christmas Eve, when we checked into our hotel in Nice, there was no Christmas spirit in our hearts.

It was raining and cold when we went out to eat. We found a drab little restaurant shoddily decorated for the holiday. Only five tables were occupied. There were two German couples, two French families, and an American sailor, by himself. In the corner a piano player listlessly played Christmas music.

I was too tired and miserable to leave. I noticed that the other customers were eating in stony silence. The only person who seemed happy was the American sailor. While eating, he was writing a letter, and a half-smile lighted his face.

My wife ordered our meal in French. The waiter brought us the wrong thing. I scolded my wife for being stupid. The boys defended her, and I felt even worse.

Then, at the table with the French family on our left, the father slapped one of his children for some minor infraction, and the boy began to cry.

On our right, the German wife began berating her husband....Through the front door came an old flower woman. She wore a dripping, tattered overcoat, and shuffled in on wet, rundown shoes. She went from one table to the other.

"Flowers, monsieur? Only one franc."

No one bought any.

Wearily she sat down at a table between the sailor and us. To the waiter she said, "A bowl of soup. I haven't sold a flower all afternoon." To the piano player she said hoarsely, "Can you imagine, Joseph, soup on Christmas Eve?"

He pointed to his empty "tipping plate."

The young sailor finished his meal and got up to leave. Putting on his coat, he walked over to the flower woman's table.

"Happy Christmas," he said, smiling and picking out two corsages. "How much are they?"

"Two francs, monsieur."

Pressing one of the small corsages flat, he put it into the letter he had written, then handed the woman a 20-franc note.

"I don't have change, monsieur," she said. "I'll get some from the waiter."

"No, ma'am," said the sailor, leaning over and kissing the ancient cheek. "This is my Christmas present to you."

Then he came to our table, holding the other corsage in front of him. "Sir," he said to me, "may I have permission to present these flowers to your beautiful daughter?"

In one quick motion he gave my wife the corsage, wished us a Merry Christmas and departed.

Everyone had stopped eating. Everyone had been watching the sailor. Everyone was silent.

A few seconds later Christmas exploded throughout the restaurant like a bomb.

The old flower woman jumped up, waving the 20-franc note, shouted to the piano player, "Joseph, my Christmas present! And you shall have half so you can have a feast too."

The piano player began to belt out *Good King Wencelaus*, beating the keys with magic hands.

My wife waved her corsage in time to the music. She appeared 20 years younger. She began to sing, and our three sons joined her, bellowing with enthusiasm.

"*Gut! Gut!*" shouted the Germans. They began singing in German.

The waiter embraced the flower woman. Waving their arms, they sang in French.

The Frenchman who had slapped the boy beat rhythm with his fork against a bottle. The lad climbed on his lap, singing in a youthful soprano.

A few hours earlier 18 persons had been spending a miserable evening. It ended up being the happiest, the very best Christmas Eve, they had ever experienced.

This, Admiral McDonald, is what I am writing you about. As the top man in the Navy, you should know about the very special gift that the U.S. Navy gave to my family, to me and to the other people in that French restaurant. Because your young sailor had Christmas spirit in his soul, he released the love and joy that had been smothered within us by anger and disappointment. He gave us Christmas.

Thank you, Sir, very much.

Merry Christmas,
Bill Lederer

BLOWIN' IN THE WIND

BOB DYLAN, 1962

How many roads must a man walk down
Before they call him a man?
Yes, 'n' how many seas must a white dove sail
Before she sleeps in the sand?
Yes, 'n' how many times must the cannon balls fly
Before they're forever banned?
The answer, my friend, is blowin' in the wind,
The answer is blowin' in the wind.

How many times must a man look up
Before he can see the sky?
Yes, 'n' how many ears must one man have
Before he can hear people cry?
Yes, 'n' how many deaths will it take till he knows
That too many people have died?
The answer, my friend, is blowin' in the wind,
The answer is blowin' in the wind.

How many years can a mountain exist
Before it's washed to the sea?
Yes, 'n' how many years can some people exist
Before they're allowed to be free?
Yes, 'n' how many times can a man turn his head,
Pretending he just doesn't see?
The answer, my friend, is blowin' in the wind,
The answer is blowin' in the wind.

I Have a Dream

Dr. Martin Luther King, Jr.
Washington, D.C., August 28, 1963

I AM HAPPY TO JOIN WITH YOU TODAY in what will go down in history as the greatest demonstration for freedom in the history of our nation.

Fivescore years ago, a great American, in whose symbolic shadow we stand today, signed the Emancipation Proclamation. This momentous decree came as a great beacon light of hope to millions of Negro slaves who had been seared in the flames of withering injustice. It came as a joyous daybreak to end the long night of their captivity.

But one hundred years later, the Negro still is not free; one hundred years later, the life of the Negro is still sadly crippled by the manacles of segregation and the chains of discrimination; one hundred years later, the Negro lives on a lonely island of poverty in the midst of a vast ocean of material prosperity; one hundred years later, the Negro is still languished in the corners of American society and finds himself an exile in his own land....

I am not unmindful that some of you have come here out of excessive trials and tribulations. Some of you have come fresh from narrow jail cells. Some of you have come from areas where your quest for freedom left you battered by the storms of persecution and staggered by the winds of police brutality. You have been the veterans of creative suffering. Continue to work with the faith that unearned suffering is redemptive.

Go back to Mississippi; go back to Alabama; go back to South Carolina; go back to Georgia; go back to Louisiana; go back to the slums and ghettos of the northern cities, knowing that somehow this situation can, and will be changed. Let us not wallow in the valley of despair.

So I say to you, my friends, that even though we must face the difficulties of today and tomorrow, I still have a dream. It is a dream deeply rooted in the American dream that one day this nation will rise up and live out the true meaning of its creed—we hold these truths to be self-evident, that all men are created equal.

I have a dream that one day on the red hills of Georgia, sons of former slaves and sons of former slave-owners will be able to sit down together at the table of brotherhood.

I have a dream that one day, even the state of Mississippi, a state sweltering with the heat of injustice, sweltering with the heat of oppression, will be transformed into an oasis of freedom and justice.

I have a dream that my four little children will one day live in a nation where they will not be judged by the color of their skin but by the content of their character. I have a dream today!

I have a dream that one day, down in Alabama, with its vicious racists, with its governor having his lips dripping with the words of interposition and nullification, one day, right there in Alabama, little black boys and black girls will be able to join hands with little white boys and white girls as sisters and brothers. I have a dream today!

I have a dream that one day every valley shall be exalted, every hill and mountain shall be made low, the rough places shall be made plain, and the crooked places shall be made straight, and the glory of the Lord will be revealed and all flesh shall see it together.

This is our hope. This is the faith that I go back to the South with.

With this faith we will be able to hear out of the mountain of despair a stone of hope. With this faith we will be able to transform the jangling discords of our nation into a beautiful symphony of brotherhood.

With this faith we will be able to work together, to pray together, to struggle together, to go to jail together, to stand up for freedom together, knowing that we will be free one day. This will be the day, this will be the day when all of God's children will be able to sing with new meaning—"my country, 'tis of thee, sweet land of liberty; of thee I sing; land where my fathers died, land of the pilgrim's pride, from every mountainside, let freedom ring"—and if America is to be a great nation, this must become true.

So let freedom ring from the prodigious hilltops of New Hampshire.

Let freedom ring from the mighty mountains of New York.

Let freedom ring from the heightening Alleghenies of Pennsylvania.

Let freedom ring from the snow-capped Rockies of Colorado.

Let freedom ring from the curvaceous slopes of California.

But not only that.

Let freedom ring from Stone Mountain of Georgia.

Let freedom ring from Lookout Mountain of Tennessee.

Let freedom ring from every hill and molehill of Mississippi, from every mountainside, let freedom ring.

And when we allow freedom to ring, when we let it ring from every village and every hamlet, from every state and every city, we will be able to speed up that day when all of God's children—black men and white men, Jews and Gentiles, Catholics and Protestants—will be able to join hands and sing in the words of the old Negro spiritual, "Free at last, free at last, thank God Almighty, we are free at last."

The South

Arkansas has the nation's only active diamond mine.

In 1836, Alabama became the first state to make Christmas an official holiday.

More than 325 motorcycles, some from as far back as 1904, are on display in North America's largest motorcycle collection, in the Barber Vintage Motorsports Museum in Birmingham, Alabama.

Disney World, in Orlando, Florida, covers 27,000 acres of land.

The rights to South Carolina's state anthem, "Carolina," belong to Michael Jackson.

Gladys Knight almost recorded "Midnight Plane to Houston," but she changed the lyrics at the last minute to "Midnight Train to Georgia" because she was from the Peach State.

The odd zigzag in the North Carolina-South Carolina state line, just south of Charlotte, was created in 1772, when boundary commissioners altered the border to avoid splitting the Catawba Indians between the two British colonies.

Charlotte, North Carolina, was the gold-mining capitol of the United States from 1788 until 1848, when gold was discovered in California.

The famous pirate Blackbeard's reign of terror ended off the coast of North Carolina in 1718. Lieutenant Robert Maynard, his vanquisher, sailed home with Blackbeard's head dangling from his ship.

Sequoyah, a North Carolina Cherokee warrior, silversmith and painter, designed an alphabet for his language in 1821. Within two years most of his people could read and write. The alphabet contained 86 letters and combined characters from English, Hebrew, and Greek.

Virginia extends 95 miles farther west than *West* Virginia.

The Virginia colony adopted the pineapple as its the symbol for hospitality. The pineapple is still used as such, found over doorways, on furniture and as centerpieces.

75 percent of West Virginia is covered in forest.

Ted Turner (1938–) founded the country's first 24-hour news channel in Atlanta in 1980. It's called Cable News Network— or CNN.

FROM

THE FEMININE MYSTIQUE

BETTY FRIEDAN, 1963

IF I AM RIGHT, the problem that has no name stirring in the minds of so many American women today is not a matter of loss of femininity or too much education, or the demands of domesticity. It is far more important than anyone recognizes. It is the key to these other new and old problems which have been torturing women and their husbands and children, and puzzling their doctors and educators for years. It may well be the key to our future as a nation and a culture. We can no longer ignore that voice within women that says: "I want something more than my husband and my children and my home."

DIVINE SECRETS OF THE YA-YA SISTERHOOD

REBECCA WELLS, 1996 (EXCERPT SET IN THE 1960s)

Oh, HOW MAMA AND THE YA-YAS LAUGHED! I could hear them from the water where I played with my brothers and my sister, Lulu, and the other Petite Ya-Yas. We'd plunge into the creek, then burst back up and hear their laughter. Caro's chortle sounded like a grin doing a polka. Teensy's giggle had a bayou flavor, as if somebody sprinkled Tabasco on it. Necie's hee-hee-hee sounded exactly like that. And Mama's head-thrown-back, open-back, open-throated roar always made people turn around and look at her when she laughed in public.

The Ya-Yas laughed a lot when they were around each other. They'd get going and not be able to stop. They'd laugh till big, fat tears rolled down their cheeks. They'd laugh until one would accuse the others of making her tee-tee in her pants. I don't know what they laughed about. I only know that their laughter was beautiful to hear and see, and that it is something I wish I had more of in my life right now. I like to pride myself on doing many things better than my mother, but she was always better at giggling with her girlfriends.

This is how the Ya-Yas used to be on the creekbank in the summers of my childhood. They'd coat their bodies with a baby-oil-and-iodine mixture, which they shook up in a big Johnson's Baby Oil bottle. The mixture was heavy, reddish-brown, an almost bloodlike tint. They'd coat their faces, arms, and legs, then take turns rubbing the solution on each other's backs.

When my mother lay down, her hands went under her chin, her head rolled to one side, her eyes closed, and she'd let out a long sigh that said how much she loved it all. I loved seeing my mother so relaxed.

This was in the days before anyone worried about skin cancer, long before rays of the sun were thought to be anything but healthy. Before we killed the ozone that stood sentry between our flesh and the sun.

Mama and Caro usually wore striped tank suits, replicas of ones they used to wear when they were lifeguards at Camp

Minnie Maddern for Southern Girls, before they married and had babies.

My mother was a beautiful swimmer. Her stroke was the Australian crawl. Watching Mama swim was like watching a woman who knew how to waltz perfectly, only her partner was not a man, but creek water. Her kick was strong, her stroke fluid, and when she rolled her head from side to side to breathe, you could barely see her mouth open. "There is no excuse for a messy swimmer, any more than there is for a messy eater," she told us. My mother judged people by how well they swam and whether they made her laugh or not.

Spring Creek was not wide like the Garnet River or huge like the Gulf of Mexico or long like some lakes. It was just a small brown body of water, well suited to mothers and children. While the creek was perfectly safe, we were warned about the areas out of sight. Out where the creek curved, where it was too deep. Past where old logs divided the swimming area from a darker, deeper one. Alligators that could eat a kid whole lived out there. They waited for bad little children who disobeyed their mothers. They crawled into your dreams at night. They could eat you, they could eat your mother, they could pull the rug out from under you when you least expected it, and then gobble you whole before you knew it.

"Even *I* can't save yall from the alligators," Mama used to say. "So don't push your luck."

When Mama swam her laps—ten times around the circumference of the swimming hole—she made the creek seem larger than it was. I marveled at her solitude as she swam those laps. She called it her "swim around the world," and I couldn't wait until my own stroke was strong enough for me to follow in her wake. Mama would conclude her swim by coming back to the shallow end, where the sandbar beach was. She'd emerge from the water, shake her head, and jump on one foot to shake the water out of her ear. Then she'd do the same on the other side. I marveled at her beauty, all wet and cool, her hair slicked back, her eyes shining, proud of her strength.

Mama and the Ya-Yas carried a big red ice chest down to the creek with them every day. The old tin kind with a lid that snapped off. Inside were chunks of ice chipped off large blocks of ice that we'd buy at the Spring Creek Shop and Skate, the local grocery and roller rink across the road from the creek.

That ice kept their beer and our Cokes cold. On top of the beer and Cokes were our ham and cheese sandwiches wrapped in wax paper. The crusts were cut off the sandwiches for the four of us, who wouldn't touch bread if the crust was left on. Paper napkins sat on top of the sandwiches, and when we opened the chest and lifted them out, they had a papery, powdery coolness that disappeared instantly, so we would quickly raise them to our cheeks as soon as we could in order to savor the chilly darkness of the ice chest.

Mama still drank beer when we were little. It was not until I was a teenager that she gave up beer altogether because it was too fattening. But even back then, when we were little, Mama would often forgo a beer in favor of a vodka and grapefruit juice, which she kept in a squat aqua-and-white thermos. Across the front of the little thermos she had written with a freezer pen: RE-VIVI-FICATION TONIC. She described the concoction as "a cocktail and diet aid rolled into one."

"FOUR LITTLE GIRLS WERE KILLED..."

CHARLES B. MORGAN, JR.
BIRMINGHAM, ALABAMA, SEPTEMBER 16, 1963

The violence over segregation in Birmingham had reached a fever pitch when, on September 15, 1963, four African-American girls attending church were killed by a bomb. The next day, local white lawyer Charles B. Morgan addressed Birmingham's Young Businessman's Club.

FOUR LITTLE GIRLS were killed in Birmingham yesterday.

A mad, remorseful worried community asks, "Who did it? Who threw that bomb? Was it a Negro or a white?" The answer should be, "We all did it." Every last one of us is condemned for that crime and the bombing before it and a decade ago. We all did it.

A short time later, white policemen kill a Negro and wound another. A few hours later, two young men on a motorbike shoot and kill a Negro child. Fires break out, and, in Montgomery, white youths assault Negroes.

And all across Alabama, an angry, guilty people cry out their mocking shouts of indignity and say they wonder "Why?" "Who?" Everyone then "deplores" the "dastardly" act.

But you know the "who" of "Who did it" is really rather simple. The "who" is every little individual who talks about the "niggers" and spreads

the seeds of his hate to his neighbor and his son. The jokester, the crude oaf whose racial jokes rock the party with laughter.

The "who" is every governor who ever shouted for lawlessness and became a law violator.

It is every senator and every representative who in the halls of Congress stands and with mock humility tells the world that things back home aren't really like they are.

It is courts that move ever so slowly, and newspapers that timorously defend the law.

It is all the Christians and all their ministers who spoke too late in anguished cries against violence. It is the coward in each of us who clucks admonitions.

We have 10 years of lawless preachments, 10 years of criticism of law, of courts, of our fellow man, a decade of telling school children the opposite of what the civics books say.

We are a mass of intolerance and bigotry and stand indicted before our young. We are cursed by the failure of each of us to accept responsibility, by our defense of an already dead institution....

Birmingham is the only city in America where the police chief and the sheriff in the school crisis had to call our local ministers together to tell them to do their duty. The ministers of

Birmingham who have done so little for Christianity call for prayer at high noon in a city of lawlessness, and in the same breath, speak of our city's "image."...

Those four little Negro girls were human beings. They have their 14 years in a leaderless city; a city where no one accepts responsibility; where everybody wants to blame somebody else. A city with a reward fund which grew like Topsy as a sort of sacrificial offering, a balm for the conscience of the "good people."...

And, who is really guilty? Each of us. Each citizen who has not consciously attempted to bring about peaceful compliance with the decisions of the Supreme Court of the United States, every citizen and every school board member and schoolteacher and principal and businessman and judge and lawyer who has corrupted the minds of our youth; every person in this community who has in any way contributed during the past several years to the popularity of hatred, is at least as guilty, or more so, than the demented fool who threw that bomb.

What's it like living in Birmingham? No one ever really has known and no one will until this city becomes part of the United States.

Birmingham is not a dying city; it is dead.

PARADOX AND DREAM

JOHN STEINBECK, 1966

ONE OF THE GENERALITIES most often noted about Americans is that we are a restless, a dissatisfied, a searching people. We bridle and buck under failure, and we go mad with dissatisfaction in the face of success. We spend our time searching for security, and hate it when we get it. For the most part we are an intemperate people: we eat too much when we can, drink too much, indulge our senses too much. Even in our so-called virtues we are intemperate: a teetotaler is not content not to drink—he must stop all the drinking in the world; a vegetarian among us would outlaw the eating of meat. We work too hard, and many die under the strain; and then to make up for that we play with a violence as suicidal.

The result is that we seem to be in a state of turmoil all the time, both physically and mentally. We are able to believe that our government is weak, stupid, overbearing, dishonest, and inefficient, and at the same time we are deeply convinced that it is the best government in the world, and we would like to impose it upon everyone else. We speak of

the American Way of Life as though it involved the ground rules for the governance of heaven. A man hungry and unemployed through his own stupidity and that of others, a man beaten by a brutal policeman, a woman forced into prostitution by her own laziness, high prices, availability, and despair—all bow with reverence toward the American Way of Life, although each one would look puzzled and angry if he were asked to define it. We scramble and scrabble up the stony path toward the pot of gold we have taken to mean security. We trample friends, relatives, and strangers who get in the way of our achieving it; and once we get it we shower it on psychoanalysts to try to find out why we are unhappy, and finally—if we have enough of the gold—we contribute it back to the nation in the form of foundations and charities.

We fight our way in, and try to buy our way out. We are alert, curious, hopeful, and we take more drugs designed to make us unaware than any other people. We are self-reliant and at the same time completely dependent. We are aggressive, and defenseless. Americans overindulge their children and do not like them; the children in turn are overly dependent and full of hate for their parents. We are complacent in our possessions, in our houses, in our education; but it is hard to find a man

or woman who does not want something better for the next generation. Americans are remarkably kind and hospitable and open with both guests and strangers; and yet they will make a wide circle around the man dying on the pavement. Fortunes are spent getting cats out of trees and dogs out of sewer pipes; but a girl screaming for help in the street draws only slammed doors, closed windows, and silence.

Now there is a set of generalities for you, each one of them canceled out by another generality. Americans seem to live and breathe and function by paradox; but in nothing are we so paradoxical as in our passionate belief in our own myths. We truly believe ourselves to be natural-born mechanics and do-it-yourself-ers. We spend our lives in motor cars, yet most of us—a great many of us at least—do not know enough about a car to look in the gas tank when the motor fails. Our lives as we live them would not function without electricity, but it is a rare man or woman who, when the power goes off, knows how to look for a burned-out fuse and replace it. We believe implicitly that we are the heirs of the pioneers; that we have inherited self-sufficiency and the ability to take care of ourselves, particularly in relation to nature. There isn't a man among us in ten thousand who knows how to butcher a cow

or a pig and cut it up for eating, let alone a wild animal. By natural endowment, we are great rifle shots and great hunters—but when hunting season opens there is a slaughter of farm animals and humans by men and women who couldn't hit a real target if they could see it. Americans treasure the knowledge that they live close to nature, but fewer and fewer farmers feed more and more people; and as soon as we can afford to we eat out of cans, buy frozen TV dinners, and haunt the delicatessens. Affluence means moving to the suburbs, but the American suburbanite sees, if anything, less of the country than the city apartment dweller with his window boxes and his African violets carefully tended under lights. In no country are more seeds and plants and equipment purchased, and less vegetables and flowers raised.

The paradoxes are everywhere: We shout that we are a nation of laws, not men—and then proceed to break every law we can if we can get away with it. We proudly insist that we base our political positions on the issues—and we will vote against a man because of his religion, his name, or the shape of his nose.

WHAT A WONDERFUL WORLD

GEORGE DAVID WEISS AND BOB THIELE, 1967

I see trees of green, red roses too,
I see them bloom for me and you,
and I think to myself
What a wonderful world.

I see skies of blue and clouds of white,
the bright blessed day, the dark sacred night,
and I think to myself
What a wonderful world.

The colors of the rainbow, so pretty in the sky
are also on the faces of people goin' by,
I see friends shakin' hands, sayin', "How do you do!"
They're really sayin', "I love you,"

I hear babies cry, I watch them grow
they'll learn much more than I'll ever know and
      I think to myself,
What a wonderful world.
Yes, I think to myself
What a wonderful world.

Strawberry Rhubarb Pie
with Meringue

O riginally viewed as a medicinal plant in ancient China, rhubarb was promoted by explorer Marco Polo in Italy and France. It arrived in the New World in the 1800s, when a Maine farmer obtained seeds from England. Combined with strawberries, it has become the filling for this classic American pie.

Pie Dough

1 ⅓ cups unbleached white flour

½ teaspoon salt

6 tablespoons chilled butter

3–4 tablespoons ice water

Filling

4 cups peeled and chopped rhubarb (approximately 6 stalks)

2 tablespoons water

¾ cup sugar

2 tablespoons cornstarch

2 cups fresh strawberries, quartered

Meringue Topping

2 egg whites, at room temperature

¼ cup sugar

1. Preheat the oven to 425°F.

2. Mix the flour and salt in a large bowl. Using a pastry cutter or two knives, cut the butter into the flour and salt until it resembles cornmeal. Be careful not to overmix.

3. One tablespoon at a time, mix in the ice water (you can use a fork or your fingers) until you can shape the dough into a ball.

4. Wrap the dough in waxed paper and refrigerate for 20 minutes.

5. Roll out the crust between two sheets of waxed paper until it's about an inch larger (all around) than your pie pan. Remove one piece of waxed paper, place the pie pan face-down on the dough and turn the whole thing over. Remove the waxed paper, press the dough evenly into the pan and crimp the edge.

6. Cover the dough with foil and use beans or rice to weigh it down. Bake for 10 minutes.

7. Remove the weights and foil and bake for another 15 minutes, until brown. Set aside. Reduce oven to 350°F.

8. In a saucepan, combine rhubarb, water, sugar and cornstarch and heat until boiling. Reduce heat and simmer 3–4 minutes. Add strawberries and simmer another couple of minutes, until soupy. Pour into a bowl and let stand in a cool place until it reaches room temperature.

9. With an electric mixer, beat the egg whites until foamy. Add sugar, 1 tablespoon at a time, and beat until glossy and stiff.

10. Pour the rhubarb mixture into the crust and pipe the meringue mixture over it in whatever design you choose. Bake for 10 minutes, until meringue is golden.

Serves 8.

COAL MINER'S DAUGHTER

LORETTA LYNN, 1969

Well, I was born a coal miner's daughter
In a cabin on a hill in Butcher Holler.
We were poor, but we had love;
That's the one thing that daddy made sure of.
He shoveled coal to make a poor man's dollar.

My daddy worked all night in the coal mine,
All day long in a field hoe-in' corn.
Mommie rocked the baby that night,
Read the Bible by a coal-oil light
And ever'thing would start all over come break of morn.

Daddy loved and raised eight kids on a coal miner's pay;
Mommie scrubbed our clothes on a washboard ev'ry day.
I've seen her fingers bleed;
To complain there was no need.
She'd smile in mommie's understanding way.

In the summer time we didn't have shoes to wear,
But in the winter time we'd all get a brand new pair.
From a mail order catalog,
Money made by selling a hog.
Daddy always managed to get money somewhere.

I'm proud to be a coal miner's daughter.
I remember well the well where I drew water.
The work we done was hard;
At night we'd sleep 'cause we were tired.
I never thought I'd ever leave Butcher Holler.

But a lot of things has changed since way back then
And it's so good to be back home again.
Not much left but the floor,
Nothin' lives here anymore.
Just a memory of a coal miner's daughter.

Odd Town Names

Humptulips

WASHINGTON

MONTANA

OREGON

Beer Bottle
Crossing

IDAHO

WYOMING

Jackpot

Chugwate

Rough and Ready

NEVADA

UTAH

Climax

COLORA

CALIFORNIA

Mexican Hat

Dunmovin

ARIZONA

NEW MEXIC

Hellhole Palms

Truth or
Consequences

ALASKA

Eek

HAWAII

Augusta, Ga.

NORTH DAKOTA

MINNESOTA

Nimrod

SOUTH DAKOTA

Porcupine

NEBRASKA

KANSAS

Buttermilk

Okay

OKLAHOMA

Noodle

TEXAS

WISCONSIN

IOWA

What Cheer

ILLINOIS

MISSOURI

Enough

Toad Suck

ARKANSAS

Darling

MISSISSIPPI

LOUISIANA

MICHIGAN

Bad Axe

Cat Elbow Corner

Normal

INDIANA

OHIO

Blue Ball

Surprise

Ordinary

KENTUCKY

Difficult

TENNESSEE

Between

Burnt Corn

Sopchoppy

ALABAMA

GEORGIA

FLORIDA

MAINE

Mosquitoville

Lost Nation

NEW
HAMPSHIRE

Bald Head

VERMONT

MASSACHUSETTS

NEW YORK

Sandwich

RHODE ISLAND

CONNECTICUT

PENNSYLVANIA

Home

NEW
JERSEY

Love Ladies

Boring

Little Heaven

MARYLAND

DELAWARE

WEST
VIRGINIA

Bumpass

VIRGINIA

Climax

NORTH
CAROLINA

Welcome

SOUTH
CAROLINA

TES

341

AMERICA

MAYA ANGELOU, 1975

THE GOLD OF HER PROMISE
    HAS NEVER BEEN MINED

HER BORDERS OF JUSTICE
    NOT CLEARLY DEFINED

HER CROPS OF ABUNDANCE
    THE FRUIT AND THE GRAIN

HAVE NOT FED THE HUNGRY
    NOR EASED THAT DEEP PAIN

HER PROUD DECLARATIONS
    ARE LEAVES ON THE WIND

HER SOUTHERN EXPOSURE
    BLACK DEATH DID BEFRIEND

DISCOVER THIS COUNTRY
    DEAD CENTURIES CRY

ERECT NOBLE TABLETS
    WHERE NONE CAN DECRY

"SHE KILLS HER BRIGHT FUTURE
    AND RAPES FOR A SOU

THEN ENTRAPS HER CHILDREN
    WITH LEGENDS UNTRUE"

I BEG YOU

DISCOVER THIS COUNTRY.

Liberty for all

Commencement Address at Lake Forest College

Dr. Seuss (Theodore Seuss Geisel)
Lake Forest, Illinois, June 4, 1977

"My Uncle Terwilliger on the Art of Eating Popovers"

My uncle ordered popovers
from the restaurant's bill of fare,
and, when they were served, he regarded them
with a penetrating stare....
Then he spoke great Words of Wisdom
as he sat there on that chair:
"To eat these things," said my uncle,
"You must exercise great care.
You may swallow down what's solid...
BUT...you must spit out the air!"

And...as you partake of the world's bill of fare,
that's darned good advice to follow.
Do a lot of spitting out the hot air.
And be careful what you swallow.

JOHN "SOUP" CAMPBELL TO EDWARD VAN EVERY, JR.

JUNE 8, 1985

Vietnam veteran John Campbell wrote this letter to Eddie Van Every, a twenty-two-year-old soldier in Campbell's company. It was left, as are so many other letters, at the Vietnam Veterans Memorial ("The Wall") in Washington, D.C.

Dear Eddie,

Although it's been fifteen years since you've been gone, it feels like it could have been fifteen days. Many times I have regretted not getting to know you better than I did. There was a quiet, sensitive goodness about you. You were one of the guys that had been with the unit awhile and was getting "short." I knew about your girl, your Mom & Dad and that you wanted to put your time in and get home. If anyone knew you at all, they liked you a lot.

I'll never forget being awakened at 3 that morning by the hysterical crying of Denny Newbill and Jerry Hall. "One of our guys is dead!" was all I could get out of Newbill. When Jerry told me it was you, I can remember demanding an answer—"Oh God, Why? Why any of us? Why Eddie?" I never did get any concrete answers. Our

346

whole company felt a tremendous loss. When I left in August, there was still a sense of grief around. Things never did get back to "normal."

I hope you don't mind, but recently I made contact with your parents. They've moved twice and are now retired in Missouri, trusting in the Lord that you are at peace. They can't afford to travel much, so I've sent them pictures of the Memorial and your name. They're good people, too. I hope to meet them some day.

For years, I felt your life, as well as the other 58,000 lives, was wasted and anyone who wasn't there, could not or would not understand what we went through. That's changing now. People are beginning to realize that we were doing our jobs and doing them well. We had to pay the price and until recently, we were the ones tagged as losers, not our government. So if your names on this wall make it harder to send guys half way around the world to die, then maybe it wasn't a total waste.

I love you, brother. I pray some day we can welcome each other home. Peace.

> *John "Soup" Campbell*
> *335th Radio Research Co.*
> *Can Tho, Vietnam*
> *Aug. 1969 to Aug. 1970*

New York

George Washington's inauguration took place on April 30, 1789, in New York City. The Big Apple enjoyed a brief stint as the nation's capitol from 1789–1790.

WASHINGTON'S INAUGURATION AS PRESIDENT

NYC is the largest city in the U.S. According to the 2000 census, 8,008,278 people live in its five boroughs.

The index finger of the Statue of Liberty in New York harbor is eight feet long.

The Empire State Building took 7 million man-hours, 1 year and 45 days (including Sundays and holidays) to build. It changes colors for special occasions and holidays, and its lights are turned off on foggy nights and during bird migration season.

Some famous New Yorkers: Lucille Ball, Steven Spielberg, Mickey Rooney, James Cagney, John D. Rockefeller, Norman Rockwell, Teddy and Franklin Roosevelt and Walt Whitman.

Who was the real Typhoid Mary? She was Mary Mallon, an Irish immigrant cook who infected 22 New Yorkers with typhoid fever from 1900–1907. When she was finally tracked down, she hid behind a row of trashcans. For the sake of public health she was kept in isolation until her death.

✳

New York City's Cathedral of St. John the Divine is the largest Gothic cathedral in the world. Under construction since 1892, the building is still only two-thirds complete.

✳

Four mountain ranges grace New York state's topography: the Adirondack, Catskill, Shawangunk, and Taconic.

✳

There are more Irish in New York City than in Dublin, more Italians than in Rome, and more Jews than in Tel Aviv.

✳

Broadway, one of the world's longest streets, runs 150 miles, from Bowling Green in lower Manhattan to the state capitol in Albany.

✳

The state insect of New York is the ladybug.

✳

America's first vending machines were installed on New York City subway platforms in 1888. They sold chewing gum.

✳

In 1905, Gennaro Lombardi opened the first pizzeria in North America on New York City's Spring Street.

CITYWIDE PRAYER SERVICE AT YANKEE STADIUM

RUDOLPH GIULIANI, SEPTEMBER 23, 2001

EVEN IN THE MIDST OF THE DARKEST TRAGEDY there are miracles that help our faith to go on. I would like to share one miracle of September 11th with you.

St. Paul's Chapel is one of the oldest and most historic buildings in the City of New York. It was built in 1766, when the surrounding area was still countryside. The Chapel survived our war of independence—including seven years of wartime occupation.

After George Washington was inaugurated the first President of the United States, in New York City on April 30th, 1789, he walked to St. Paul's, and he kneeled down to pray. The pew where he worshipped is still there. Framed on the wall beside it is the oldest known representation of the Great Seal of the United States of America—it's a majestic eagle, holding in one talon an olive branch, proclaiming our abiding desire for peace...and in the other, a cluster of arrows, a forewarning of our determination to defend our liberty. On a banner above the Eagle is written *E Pluribus Unum*, "Out of Many, One."

For the past twenty-five years, the chapel stood directly in the shadow of the World Trade Center Towers. When the Towers fell, more than a dozen modern buildings were destroyed and damaged. Yet somehow, amid all the destruction and devastation, St. Paul's Chapel still stands...without so much as a broken window.

It's a small miracle in some ways, but the presence of that chapel standing defiant and serene amid the ruins of war sends an eloquent message about the strength and resilience of the people of New York City, and the people of America.

We unite under the banner of *E Pluribus Unum*. We find strength in our diversity. We're a city where people look different, talk different, think different. But we're a city at one with all of the people at the World Trade Center, and with all of America. We love our diversity, and we love our freedom.

Like our founding fathers who fought and died for freedom...like our ancestors who fought and died to preserve our union and to end the sin of slavery...like our fathers and grandfathers who fought and died to liberate the world from Nazism, and Fascism, and Communism...the cluster of arrows to defend our freedom, and the olive branch of peace have now been handed to us.

We will hold them firmly in our hands, honor their memory, and lift them up toward heaven to light the world.

In the days since this attack, we have met the worst of humanity with the best of humanity.

1896	First motion picture demonstration in the U.S. held in New York City
	Supreme Court establishes "separate but equal" doctrine in *Plessy v. Ferguson*
1898	Spanish-American War begins over Cuba; ends with Spain ceding Cuba,
	Puerto Rico, Guam, Philippines to the U.S. for $20 million
1900	Hurricane whips through Galveston, Texas, killing more than 6,000
1901	Anarchist assassinates President William McKinley;
	Theodore Roosevelt assumes presidency
1903	First official baseball World Series Championship; more than 100,000 attend
	Wright brothers fly the 1st motorized airplane
	First crossing of American continent by car: 65 days coast-to-coast
1906	San Francisco earthquake and fire leaves 3,000 dead, 225,000 homeless,
	28,000 buildings destroyed
1908	First Model T Ford assembled in Detroit
1909	Multiracial group of activists form National Negro Committee (later renamed National
	Association for the Advancement of Colored People)
1912	*Titanic* sinks; 1,503 dead
1913	16th Amendment establishes permanent income tax
	Cecil B. DeMille shoots 1st Hollywood full-length feature, *The Squaw Man*
1914	WWI ignites in Europe
1915	German U-Boat sinks passenger ship *Lusitania*; 128 Americans are among 1,198 dead
1916	Jeannette Rankin becomes 1st U.S. Congresswoman
	Margeret Sanger opens 1st U.S. birth control clinic in Brooklyn, New York
1917	U.S. joins Allies in WWI, declaring war on Germany
1918	Armistice declared (on 11th hour of 11th day of 11th month), ending the war
1919	Treaty of Versailles signed by Allies and Germans
1920	Following 18th Amendment (ratified 1919), America enters Prohibition
	19th Amendment adopted, giving American women the right to vote
1924	10 millionth Ford motorcar produced
1925	F. Scott Fitzgerald publishes *The Great Gatsby*
1927	Charles Lindbergh flies nonstop NY—Paris in *The Spirit of St. Louis* (33.5 hours)
	First "talkie": *The Jazz Singer* with Al Jolson
	Babe Ruth hits 60 homers for the NY Yankees
1928	Mickey Mouse debuts in Disney's *Steamboat Willie*
1929	Hollywood hosts 1st Academy Awards
	October 28: Stock Exchange collapses, U.S. plunges into Great Depression

1932	Amelia Earhart makes 1st female solo flight across the Atlantic
1933	Joseph Strauss begins 4-year construction of San Francisco's Golden Gate Bridge
	Franklin Delano Roosevelt elected 32nd president; his New Deal gets America back to work
1935	Roosevelt signs Social Security Act
1937	Amelia Earhart's plane disappears during Pacific flight
1939	World War II ravages Europe
1940	John Steinbeck's 1939 novel *The Grapes of Wrath* wins Pulitzer Prize
1941	Completion of Mt. Rushmore monument
	December 7: Japanese planes bomb Pearl Harbor
	December 8: U.S. declares war on Japan, entering WWII; declarations against Germany and Italy follow shortly
1944	June 6: D-Day: General Dwight D. Eisenhower leads massive assault on Nazi-occupied France
1945	August 6 & 9: U.S. drops atomic bombs on Hiroshima and Nagasaki, Japan soon surrenders, ending war
1946	First U.S. nuclear weapons effects tests, Bikini Atoll
1948	Congress passes $17 billion Marshall Plan to rebuild Europe, tensions between Soviet communists and Allied democracies signal beginning of Cold War
1949	North Atlantic Treaty Organization (NATO) created among Western nations
	U.S. market in television sets reaches $1.5 million
1950	3-year Korean War begins after North Korean troops invade South Korea with Russian tanks
	U.S. market in television sets reaches $15 million
	Ray Bradbury publishes *The Martian Chronicles*
1954	Supreme Court ends school segregation and overturns "separate but equal" doctrine in *Brown v. Board of Education*
	Nationwide testing of Jonas Salk's polio vaccine
1956	Blacks in Montgomery, Alabama, stage bus boycott
1959	Hawaii is the 50th and last state admitted to the Union
1960	John F. Kennedy elected President
1961	U.S.-sponsored Cuban exiles conduct failed Bay of Pigs invasion of Cuba
1962	U.S.-Soviet showdown over Cuban Missile Crisis, J.F.K. and Premier Nikita Kruschev narrowly avert nuclear war
1963	Lee Harvey Oswald assassinates President Kennedy in Dallas, Texas; Lyndon B. Johnson assumes presidency
	Civil rights demonstrations meet with violence in Birmingham, Alabama
	Betty Friedan publishes *The Feminine Mystique*
1964	Beatles appear on Ed Sullivan show, Beatlemania grips America